TEXAS BBQ
ADVENTURE GUIDE

A ROAD TRIP THROUGH THE HISTORY &
HOW-TO OF LONE STAR 'QUE

JASON WEEMS

AMERICAN PALATE

Published by American Palate
A Division of The History Press
Charleston, SC
www.historypress.com

Front cover, clockwise from top left: Charlie's BBQ in Beaumont; C&J Barbeque in Bryan; LJ's BBQ in Brenham; 2M Barbecue in San Antonio.
Back cover, top: Joe Marino Jr., owner and pitmaster of Bill's BBQ in Kerrville; *bottom*: Salt Lick BBQ in Driftwood.
All images are by the author unless otherwise noted.

First published 2022

Manufactured in the United States

ISBN 9781467150897

Library of Congress Control Number: 2022943545

Notice: The information in this book is true and complete to the best of our knowledge. It is offered without guarantee on the part of the author or The History Press. The author and The History Press disclaim all liability in connection with the use of this book.

This book is dedicated to my family and my beloved community of friends for your lifelong love and support of me and my creative endeavors.

*Also, to all those future BBQ heroes in the making.
May you draw from the passions of those (too often nameless) pitmasters and culinary alchemists who came before you and use their legacy as an inspiration to continue the evolution of this great cuisine.*

CONTENTS

ACKNOWLEDGEMENTS

I want to share my appreciation for everyone who inspired my adventure around Texas with destination suggestions, to all those who brainstormed with me about what sorts of fun could be had with this guide and to the many who feasted with me along the way for the research portion of this book. While that list is far too long to recite in totality, each of you has my deepest and most sincere gratitude for sharing in this experience with me.

I do feel compelled to give a special note of thanks to one person in particular, and that's Mr. PJ Oehler. The constant, unwavering support that he and his family have shown to me was instrumental to the success of this endeavor. His tasteful, sage guidance to me as a friend and to the book as a consultant was invaluable at every turn, and this guide might never have come to fruition without him. Thank you, PJ. I hope we have many more adventures to come.

As I raced toward, and then anxiously past, a few deadlines, there was another friend who came to the rescue in a different way. I'm referring now to Margaret Spencer, who graciously offered her assistance with pre-editing my initial manuscripts into something worthy of sharing with you, dear reader. This helping hand was a real boon to the final form that you see before you and is vastly better for her keen eye and helpful insights, as well as for the often hilarious notes she left for me to find in the margins.

Along those lines, I would also like to thank the entire team at The History Press and Arcadia Publishing, especially Ben Gibson, my commissioning editor, who has been a patient guide to me as I've journeyed deeper into the world of authorship. I look forward to the many creations and collaborations that are still to come.

A final acknowledgement and expression of gratitude that I want to make is of a more historic yet still very personal nature. Like so many of our nation's most beloved cultural treasures, such as most genres of our popular music, it can be confidently stated that barbecue was gifted to the world from the contributions, traditions and innovations of one group of Americans more than any other. Here, I refer to the brilliant chefs and pitmasters of the Black community, who, for so many generations, endured the bonds of enslavement and family separation while being held in a hostile environment. Yet despite those conditions, these brave people somehow transmuted that unimaginable pain into a cuisine that has long been synonymous with celebration and an expression of community. The feat of alchemy that we witness in the stories of these men and women is something that can serve as an inspiration to us all. To all those pitmasters, especially the ones whose tales have been lost in the fog of time, I offer my thanks and gratitude to you and your family legacies. Every fan of this food owes a debt to your unparalleled contributions to the culture and cuisine of Texas BBQ and for the inspiration of your indominable spirit.

INTRODUCTION

Welcome to the *Texas BBQ Adventure Guide*, where you'll learn to get the very most out of your barbecue experience. As a lifelong Texan, backyard grill master and lover of Texas barbecue, I know this is a cuisine that offers many styles, flavors and destinations to explore. All restaurants and regions have some similarities at their core, but the differences abound. From back-road barbecue barns to big-city craft barbecue spots with a line around the block, you're about to get the secrets and tips to successfully set off on the barbecue-centric adventure of your dreams. With this guide, you'll be able to plan a perfect barbecue trip around the Lone Star State, where you'll find all your next favorite hidden gems or simply learn how to add barbecue to your next Texas road trip while avoiding the dead ends and make it the highlight of your adventure. Perhaps best of all, you'll uncover the deeper history of Texas-style barbecue that has often gone overlooked, which will make each bite a little juicier.

I'd like to admit that to even attempt to write a book that encompasses all of Texas barbecue is a futile task. Instead, the approach of this guide will be to use the story of my travels pursuing the best of the state's offerings to give you the tools that you'll need to get the most out of your own barbecue adventures. You may be wondering what there is to learn. Well, maybe more than you'd guess! I took a series of trips around Texas in preparation for this project, and when I parked the car at the end of that last leg, I was certain of two things. First, that I needed a nap, and second, that there will always be more to learn about Texas barbecue.

Speaking a bit more about my own big barbecue tour that so informs this book, for research purposes, I traveled about 3,500 miles on several excursions over the course of ten weeks, and over those miles, I saw some of the most breathtaking beauty and met some of the kindest people this world has to offer. I ate at over thirty very different, all welcoming and most delectable barbecue restaurants in the state (sometimes up to five in a day) and delivered many pounds of leftovers and more than a few restaurant koozies to friends and family along the way. I learned the most by talking to pitmasters, the folks who run the registers and, of course, the local regulars.

I also spent a fair bit of time chasing down the history of barbecue because, to be honest, the popular narrative that we've long been told—that story of barbecue coming to us from the old West cowboys and their chuckwagons out on the cattle trail—is, at best, far from accurate and omits some of the most relevant parts of the tale. The more I traveled, read and gabbed with those locals and pitmasters, the more I found that the popular narrative I'd always been told just wouldn't hold water (or barbecue sauce, for that matter). Throughout this guide, I'll do my best to help unravel that history and set the story straight along the way.

That brings up another point regarding my research for this guide; in addition to utilizing academic resources and speaking with pitmasters and barbecue restaurateurs all over the state, I was also most fortunate to have a dialogue and interview with the BBQ editor of the vaunted *Texas Monthly Magazine*, Daniel Vaughn. Here's some context for the uninitiated reader: *TMM* curates a yearly edition of its magazine that focuses on Texas barbecue. That issue is widely regarded as the definitive go-to source of the barbecue hotspots in Texas each year. It offers adventurers like you and me resources such as a "Meat Map" that plots out this annual top 50 list. The list is unranked with a small exception; there is a ranked top 10 list chosen from the rest. If a joint can land one of those top 10 slots and be acknowledged as first among equals, it can be a business-bumping honor. Though, in truth, if any business has made it that far, the word about it has already likely gotten out. After all, it's hard to keep great barbecue a secret in Texas for long.

Vaughn curates that big list and manages the army of contributors who help assemble it. As the man at the center of the effort, there's no one else around with as keen an eye on the current and future state of this cuisine as him. His efforts steering that Texas top 50 is in addition to the significant historical research he performs for his regularly printed articles, not to mention his constant barbecue-tasting adventures as an acclaimed judge and critic. Daniel may well be the busiest man in the biz, and he has clearly earned his spot as the Kingmaker of Texas Barbecue.

I mentioned Daniel's well-researched articles on the history of barbecue, and that's what really led me to contact him. Those articles fill up countless tabs on my computer when I do my digging, so I knew there could really be no better source for clearing up my historical understanding of our subject. I reached out to him for a chat, and he was kind enough to respond. After some email exchanges where he graciously forwarded a few relevant research links for me to investigate, we spoke on a video call for nearly an hour, truly nerding out over the finer points of the Texas barbecue story the whole time. His encyclopedic knowledge of the topic was endlessly helpful to my deep dive into our subject, and the clarity gained from that exchange will come up throughout this guide. This book certainly owes a debt of gratitude for his perspective on the topic and his willingness to share his insights.

You can see that a lot has gone into how I came to write this guide, and it's my hope that by the end, you'll have a solid understanding of this complex meal that was made from so many historic ingredients and traditions. Before we dig into the history, and before you head out on that long drive to your first few barbecue destinations, there are three main things to consider right out of the gate.

First, and this may go without saying, but barbecue is quite popular, and these restaurants are often busy. What may come as a surprise, and possibly an unwelcome one at that, is that they also usually keep to their own schedules. You've got to know going in that if you don't do a little research into the best days and times for a visit and plan your trip accordingly, you may not have the experience you were hoping for. There are many ways that barbecue joints may differ from other types of restaurants, but the hours they keep is surely one of the big ones, a pretty good reason to do a little research first. For example, some only operate on the weekends, and it's a common practice to take Mondays off. A beloved haunt may only open on seemingly random days, and it will often sell out of its menu and close up shop well before dinner. All of this is to say that many of the best barbecue restaurants are doing what works for their crew and the locals, so they are rarely committed to being open until 9:00 p.m., seven days a week. They're often smaller operations, and they neither want nor, frankly, do they need to follow a traditional restaurant schedule. You can usually count on most of these restaurants to be open as a weekend lunch spot, and that also means you might be met with a line out the door or down the block. It's best to assume there's going to be some detail or other that you'll want to know before you make the journey, so get into the practice of starting each trip by checking websites and social media pages ahead of your trip to get the best and most up-to-date information. Your new favorite place for barbecue may be some food truck with a smoker trailer outside a brewery or maybe a shack off a dirt road crowded with locals and replete with taxidermized hunting trophies on every wall; you'll just never know until you try. But to get your taste of the best, you'll have to know their rules and play by them. So, to recap—since timing is everything and knowledge is power, you should always do a little research before you go.

The second thing to keep in mind when you really start to dive deeper into exploring the world of Texas barbecue is that even though we are dividing the state into five main regions, we can simplify things a bit by identifying three main styles of barbecue that have come to define the food. East Texas, South Texas and Central Texas are the main regional flavors that we find. It's from the blending of all three of those styles that we get the barbecue of Coastal Texas, and it's with the blending of Central Texas style with flavors of the South Texas style that we get the barbecue of West Texas. The tales of how these flavors mixed and came to define their regions are fascinating, and we'll be delving into those styles and their histories at length. At this modern stage in the evolution of the cuisine, you'll find the influences from one region will often show up on the menus from another, but despite the subtle merging of menus, the flavors are still distinct and unique, and each is worthy of your attention.

On a related note, it might raise an eyebrow that in my regional map, I'm omitting North Texas as its own separate area, even though two of the largest cities in the nation—Dallas and Fort Worth—are located there. Instead, we allow the line between the East and West Texas regions to continue a not-so-straight path all the way up to the Red River. For our purposes, that northern part of the border between East and West Texas partitions the city of Dallas itself, which is a decision that deserves an explanation since no one would really consider Dallas a city in East Texas. While it's true you can find all the regional barbecue styles represented in that thriving metropolis, it's the Black-owned barbecue restaurants that have come to define the local flavors of South and East Dallas. The barbecue spots in these parts are spectacular, and the menus more closely reflect the offerings of Beaumont than the offerings of any other part of the Metroplex. Meanwhile, in places such as the North Dallas suburb of McKinney or in the Cow-Town of Fort Worth, the heavy hitters are much more aligned with the influences of the West Texas region. It's because of these important subtleties that we've divided

Dallas and placed the south and east parts of the city into the East Texas region, while the North and West Dallas areas, along with Fort Worth and then on and on westward, fall into the West Texas region.

With that explanation in mind, you can see that if we understand the three main Texas barbecue styles—East, South and Central—and their influence over the other regions, and especially if we can get a feel for the context of the story behind the bites, then we'll be able to read any plate of barbecue that sits before us as if it were a delicious book.

The third consideration that you should factor into your plans is that, as I mentioned earlier, there are a lot of very different dining options available for you to dive into. This point goes beyond the basic regional styles or flavors and more into the atmosphere of the meal. Whether you're searching for a specific type of dining experience or simply open to any adventure, it helps to be aware of the options. As a way of slicing up this giant subject into more bite-sized pieces, let's first divide all the myriad barbecue dining options into two simple groups: celebration barbecue and restaurant barbecue.

Celebration barbecue is the original experience, and this cuisine is especially well suited for feeding a large crowd. We'll go into the deep connection of this food to a variety of traditions later in the book, but for now, suffice it to say that whether it's a religious gathering like Easter, a celebration of freedom such as Juneteenth or a barbecue competition at the local rodeo, celebration barbecue is one of the most historically authentic ways to enjoy this feast food.

As for restaurant barbecue, today we find a huge variety of options, and that's brought a constant level of accessibility to a cuisine that was once enjoyed exclusively as a feast or celebration food. Over time, the original barbecue restaurant archetypes emerged, and, from those, new archetypes have evolved.

Atmosphere matters when dining, and that's especially true with this cuisine. If you want a fine dining experience with barbecue, you can absolutely have it, white linen tablecloths and all, but you're not going to find it at a food truck or a meat market. You can certainly get a five-star-quality meal in those places, but the fine china plate will be replaced by a square of brown butcher paper torn off a roll.

Knowing which archetypal category a restaurant you're planning to visit falls into, and what you can expect to find in that type *before* you get there, will go a long way toward maximizing your barbecue enjoyment. These wide-ranging archetypes are another subject we'll visit throughout this guide, but the main takeaway for now is that barbecue dining experiences vary greatly, and that's a fact that I hope stokes your curiosity. Understanding the different types of offerings is a great way to get a sense for what might be in store for your visit before you make a long drive. Once you know what's out there, and which of those styles you like best, you can begin planning the perfect excursions.

That's not too bad, right? Do a little research so you can arrive at the right time, identify what kind of regional style or hybrid regional flavor style your picks are offering and know which archetype of barbecue joint you're heading out to before you arrive—get those three pieces of info, and you'll always have the makings of a great barbecue adventure.

We're barely getting started and we can already see that Texas-style barbecue is more than just a plate of meat and sides. It's the story of the people who have made it and evolved it and loved it for generations on end. It's the story of Texas, and to know our story is to know ourselves. There's perhaps no better or more honest witness to our time in this world than our food traditions and how they came to be. Barbecue is a wonderful example of that living legacy.

The full history of barbecue is one that spans the furthest depths of the time of man. Luckily for us, with our topic being Texas barbecue, we can narrow our focus a bit. Still, as I've dug into this history, even I was surprised at the breadth of the subject and the expanse of time that it covers. Our tale would be best served with a preface. As we've mentioned when discussing our five regions, barbecue is a fusion food that emerged, as is the case with most cuisines, when different cultures blended, clashed or did both. Even though barbecue brings us all together today, it hasn't always been a story of unity. In fact, this story is as messy and saucy as a pile of ribs, because it's also a tangible record of the influence and cohabitation of very different people and cultures over a long period.

Texas barbecue has many flavors and sub-styles, but its history, just like its present regional-style mainstays, could be described as a tree with three main branches. Just like our main flavors, these branches represent the regions of East Texas, South Texas and, later, Central Texas. These are absolutely the regions that most clearly define the cuisine, but the story doesn't even start in Texas. Instead, if we start at the root of the tree, we begin on the island of Haiti or, as it was called by Columbus at the time, Hispaniola.

The word *barbecue* is said to have come to us from an Indigenous Caribbean tribe of Hispaniola, the Taino people. This tribe prepared meat, such as fish or turtle, on raised racks made of green wood sitting atop a shallow bed of glowing coals. In a boucan, the green wood ensures that the rack doesn't turn to flame, but it does smolder and smoke. Soon, the meat drippings start to flavor that smoke, and the result is delicious. They called this style of cooking *barbacoa*, and the Spanish colonizers first chronicled that specific word in a book in 1526. The word may not have been written down until then, but written descriptions and accounts of this unique Taino cooking method date all the way back to Columbus's first time on the island in 1492, and that's where we find our first spark. That's the first case of "East meets West" that we can point to in this region, and though there's much more to be said on the subject, right out of the gate it produces the first hints of what would become one of the world's favorite foods.

As people came en masse to the New World, our story takes on multiple threads at nearly the same moment, but let's begin with this one: there's a specific word for those racks that were used to cook barbacoa. They were called *boucans* or *buccans*, which, not incidentally, is where we get the word "buccaneer." The buccaneers were English, Dutch or French sailors who had either been marooned and were sustaining themselves off boucan-smoked food or, if they still had a ship of their own, they usually came into possession of it by way of mutiny. They raided Spanish colonies and plundered Spanish treasure vessels, and they just happened to be quite handy with a boucan. Sometimes their violence was self-motivated, sometimes they were for hire, so whether you called them pirates or privateers simply depended on which side of their cannons—versus which side of their ledgers—you landed on.

The buccaneers who could push out from their pirate coves hidden among the Caribbean islands were even said to have sold their popular barbacoa as a side hustle in all the ports of the Caribbean Sea, the Gulf of Mexico and all over the Americas. Along with their treasures and doubloons, they took this newly born fusion food wherever the winds carried them. This subculture of the buccaneers died out as the world changed around them, but it is true that both metaphorically and somewhat literally speaking, one of the first groups that we can identify as a root of Texas barbecue was none less than pirates.

It wasn't just those swashbuckling buccaneers who had an interest in the Caribbean islands and their people. They were, after all, mostly stealing the treasures of Spain. Spain was betting heavily on exploring and colonizing this new world, and they were intent on squeezing every resource and especially every drop of gold out of the continent that they could, which takes lots of labor. It was at this point that the Native people of the Caribbean islands became enslaved by the Spanish. When the number of Indigenous slaves could no longer keep up with the demand for workers, we see these human traffickers begin to abduct and funnel in huge numbers of enslaved men and women from West Africa to toil along with the Native Americans of the West Indies.

The West Indies, especially Hispaniola and Cuba, would become the main ports of call in the New World for Spain, where explorers and colonizers would land after their trans-Atlantic voyage, as it was here that they held their seat of government for the region. So incoming ships would check in with the powers that be, gather all their supplies (and to them, "supplies" would have included an enslaved labor force) and then set off for their various attempts to conquer the Americas, such as one of the first attempts to colonize an area right between what we call North and South Carolina. It was an ill-fated attempt made by Lucas Vásquez de Ayllón in the year 1526.

Ayllón, who had arrived in the West Indies all the way back in 1502, had become a man of renown among his peers, and this being the exciting, swashbuckling frontier for the time, he got his share of press coverage back home in Spain. By 1520, he had worked out a way to advance his dream of becoming more rich, powerful and famous than even Cortes. He had received the support of the Spanish crown to mount a massive expedition to carve out a new colony, and he promptly began checking out locations along the Eastern Seaboard of North America. When he was scouting out the area between the Carolinas, he met, beguiled and invited a group of 150 curious Indigenous people from the area to check out his ship. Once they were on board, he set sail without their consent. Ayllón had kidnapped the entire group so that he could take them back to the West Indies, where he would try to indoctrinate them into slavery with the intent of using the tribe as both guides and forced labor—alongside abducted West Africans purchased from the slave markets of the Caribbean Islands.

Ayllón's colonial ambitions were ill fated, and without delving too deeply down the rabbit hole, we can note a few important things that happened in the narrative. First, not surprisingly, the 150 Native Americans who had been abducted and supposedly indoctrinated immediately left without a trace. Then, after a series of other setbacks, including the death of Ayllón, there was a slave revolt that destroyed any hope of returning the colony to self-sustainability. With that blow and the growing list of casualties among the colonists, plus the rapid onset of a deadly winter chill, the last 150 out of 600 settlers abandoned the enslaved people and left to race for their lives back to the West Indies. Most of them died of exposure and starvation along the way. It was here, at this failed colony, that most historians cite as the location of the first proper barbecue pits being made on American soil by the abandoned West Africans using the techniques created during the time spent in the slave camps of Hispaniola.

This experience of enslavement and human trafficking that was endured by and shared between Indigenous Americans, Indigenous West Indians and Indigenous West Africans is where we find the true merging of cultures that brings us barbecue. These groups would also have shared similar subsistence hunting and food preservation techniques, despite the ocean that separated their respective cultural development.

During colonization, the Spanish imported and abandoned pigs all over the Americas and the Caribbean Islands, inadvertently giving these people access to pork. Historians have debated when the boucan rack was abandoned in favor of waist-deep, square holes lined with coals, but many think it was with this addition of pork.

A hog has entirely different cooking requirements than a net full of fish. Fish are just fine raised up off the shallow bed of coals on a rack and left to slowly cook in just the magic of the smoke; in fact, that's the perfect way to do it. But you can't expect to get a good (or non-life-threatening) result using that indirect cooking technique with a whole hog. Undercooked pork can be deadly, so if you want to be safe, you need to get the meat as close to and as surrounded by the heat source as you possibly can. Losing the rack and deepening the pit to create a simple oven was the next natural and logical evolutionary step for this style of cooking. This is the likely genesis of the "plantation-style" barbecue technique that came to define southern barbecue.

The hand-dug pit technique would be shared among the enslaved people held in the market camps of the West Indies, and it traveled with them to the plantations of the American South. The few accounts of former slaves that are still available to us today record the same pit barbecue technique being used across the board in nearly all southern plantations. This, at a time before easy access to communication and in a population that was forced into illiteracy, tells us this technique was passed down in person and that it likely happened in the West Indies and early Spanish colonies where these Indigenous populations endured enslavement together and, in the process, inadvertently created southern barbecue.

Plantation-style pit barbecue is one of the most efficient and delicious ways of feeding a large group of people, so naturally, it became a celebratory meal. In time, traditions including side dishes and sauces emerged from the kitchens of enslaved chefs over the generations of life in the antebellum South. The sauce is a crucial element of African American barbecue. Reports say the original sauces would have come down to us from traditional West African recipes and were a mix of citrus juices, spices and, later, peppers.

There's a false narrative that the enslaved were frequently fed poor cuts of meat and would have commonly basted meat in barbecue sauces. This assumption would lead us to think barbecue was a regular part of the plantation laborer's diet, but that's simply not true. It may be the case that these sauces would have been used on the rare occasions that spices presented themselves, but even the worst cuts of meat were more than the average enslaved person was afforded. Most freedmen accounts recall only a poor-quality type of salted bacon as their regular ration of protein, which was not a cut of meat that would be basted and roasted.

By the time the enslaved men and women from West Africa had been trafficked to the plantations of America, barbecue had become a purely celebratory fare. As such, it was only prepared when there was a need to feed a whole group of people one giant meal. Somewhat cruelly, the holiday that plantation owners would allow the enslaved to observe was the Fourth of July. The plantation owners would take the best cuts of meat and then become spectators at the festivities and even demand to be entertained by the enslaved men, women and children at the parties. For all intents and purposes, and for a very long time, in much of America Independence Day was known almost exclusively and ironically as a holiday for the enslaved.

According to the accounts of freedmen, on this day, the plantation owners in a region would gather in one place. Each group of enslaved laborers would be given a whole hog or perhaps some other animal, such as a goat, to roast for their attendees. In a sense, the first barbecue competitions emerged as a plantation master would urge each group of cooks to rush to finish the laborious preparations required for pit barbecue and, in doing so, be the first to bring those choicest cuts of meat over to the plantation-owning family, thus winning bragging rights for the white families among their slave-holding peers.

The enslaved West Africans were sometimes allowed, on this one day, to join in the group songs and dances that harkened back to their shared tribal past, providing those enslaved men and women with some of the only interactions outside the plantation and the only traditions they were allowed to observe all year. It was a major occasion, a huge celebration, and like so much of our shared past, there's a shadow of pain that accompanied the joy.

In this view of plantation barbecue, we see there wasn't any one person who would have been using a barbecue pit or smokehouse every day. While surely some people were known to be better cooks than others, pitmasters in this era would have been opportunistically chosen from whomever was present at the time of need, and those temporary chefs relied on a communal knowledge to guide them. We won't see the rise of the true pitmasters, or access to barbecue in a ready-to-order sort of way, until much later in our story.

EAST TEXAS STYLE REGION

HOME OF THE TEXAS PINEY FOREST & BIG THICKET

WESTERNMOST REACH OF THE HISTORIC "DEEP SOUTH"

REGIONAL SPECIALTY
- PORK
- BOUDIN
- BEEF LINKS
- CAJUN & CREOLE SPICES/SIDES

ALLEGED HOME OF THE TEXAS SASQUATCH

PART I

EAST TEXAS–STYLE REGION

The history of the plantation barbecue tradition is as innovative as it is tragic in its roots, and clearly, its contribution to the evolution of this cuisine is nothing less than foundational, but how does it connect us to the story of Texas-style barbecue? It's simple, really, and the answer gets us into the first part of our adventure, so here it is—over time, the land-hungry American plantations expanded farther south and west, eventually into the region known as Texas. Since the settlement of Texas occurred from east to west, the first of these plantations were built in the east. These plantations were directly linked to the ones that came before them, and the enslaved labor force that was brought to build Texas also brought its traditions, especially celebratory barbecue. As such, you can think of East Texas as the westernmost point of the Deep South, which isn't confusing at all, right?

That's why this part of our story, this history of plantation-style barbecue, is leading us directly to the East Texas branch of our tree. As a result of that direct lineage, the barbecue that we find in this part of Texas is the most closely related to the original. Even though the technology and recipes have evolved over time, and even though the food has taken on some of the flavors of its neighbors—such as the Cajun spices and sides of Louisiana or the dry rubs, sides and beef cuts of the Hill Country—East Texas barbecue remains true to its deeply held traditions and beloved recipes.

East Texas is said to lie behind the Piney Curtain, which is to say that it's an isolated culture unto itself. But to understand how that could even be the case when it's just a portion of one state, let's gain a little perspective. Texas, being such a large territory, has several regions besides East Texas, and each one hosts vast differences within. A lot of folks believe that Texas had the right to secede from the Union if it chose to, but that's a myth. What is true is that Texans could vote to split the state into five smaller ones, and even if we did break up the band, each new state would still represent some of the largest land areas and populations in the country. Since we're already heading that way, let's use East Texas as our example. That thirty-eight-county region is a little under ten thousand square miles, which means if it were on its own, it would outsize ten smaller states. Its population as a region comes in at 1.9 million people, which would make it somewhere around the thirty-seventh-largest state by that metric. Still, when you realize that 1.9 million people is slightly less than the size of the Austin Metro population and compare that data to the Texas population of 29 million and counting, you start to see that East Texas, as a region, really is quite sparsely inhabited. Despite the way I've mapped out the flavor regions to include South and East Dallas, in truth there are only two proper East Texas cities that beat the 100,000-person mark, and those towns are Tyler on the far north side of the region and, 250 miles away, Beaumont on the far south side. Great distance being a constant factor in planning any Texas barbecue adventure, I chose to visit East Texas on two separate portions of my journey, but we'll explore it in one go for this chapter.

Since there are so few major population centers in this region, and since the region is naturally isolated by its geography, East Texas has remained a mystery to many of us big-city Texans. City-slickers like me generally accept that sometimes business or pleasure will take us to DFW, Austin, Houston or San Antonio, but you don't often casually wind up on the eastern side of the state, unless you count stopping for gas as you're passing through, because that big concert you're dying to go to or that work conference you're expected to attend isn't likely to be held in Nacogdoches. That's not to say those fine folks can't throw a party; in fact, nothing could be further from the truth.

If asked to describe the region, most Texans in the know would likely think of the great Piney Woods, which is understandable since it covers around 23,500 square miles, including parts of Louisiana and Arkansas, but that's hardly all there is to it. To risk oversimplifying the geography, a majority of the northernmost two-thirds of this region is made up of those Piney Woods sitting atop rolling hills. Mixed into those woods on the far east side of the center of the region is the "Big Thicket" or "Deep East Texas," a sub-region where the creeks and rivers drain into the forest and where we find the moss-covered cypress bayous and lakes of Texas, along with a stunning amount of biodiversity among its eleven different ecosystems. Some folks even believe there's a relic hominoid living in those piney thickets. You may not believe in Bigfoot, but that's okay. Folks around these parts know different, and for a price, they'll take you out to hear some whistles and wood-knocks. Who knows? Perhaps you can tempt them out in the open with an offering of barbecue. Beyond that mysterious land, the southern third consists of flat, grassy, coastal plains that lead down to the shores of the Gulf Coast.

CHAPTER 1

BEAUMONT

My first excursion into the region took me through those grassy coastal plains to the southeastern port of Beaumont. I knew about the barbecue traditions present in East Texas, but I really had no idea what I was in for or how different the flavors would be from the Austin and Hill Country style that I'd become so accustomed to. Historically speaking, racial lines and segregation have created generations of separation and isolation of cultures in most parts of Texas. Regarding barbecue, this isolation has allowed certain styles to be preserved and allowed others to emerge, such as we find in Beaumont.

As a port town, Beaumont has always been home to an ethnically diverse population that represents many immigrant and minority groups. According to the 2020 census, at nearly 48 percent of the citizenry, the majority ethnic group in the town is its Black community. Beaumont, like most places in the South, has a long and difficult history of racial tension, and the scars of that struggle remain visible to this day. You can see it in the more economically depressed neighborhoods of Beaumont, and not coincidentally, this is also where you will find some of the most amazing barbecue offerings in all of Texas.

Before you rush to judge the parts of town where the treasures can be found, at least know there are some very real reasons for the run-down look of the area. The Black community of Beaumont, like so many Black Meccas in the South, was thriving in the early 1900s, and for decades wealth and abundance had been built by the Black residents of the town. In 1943, amid a rising tide of racial tensions nationwide, a violent incident aimed at the Black community sparked a relentless two-day assault on these people, their homes and especially their businesses. The decimation of Black life and wealth was swift and thorough. Remember that this was the Jim Crow era, and because of the policies of the day, the victims of the attack had little to no recourse in the justice system, and on top of that, they weren't offered access to the capital needed to rebuild after the attack. With that in mind, it's understandable, though tragic, that we see long-abandoned storefronts in the neighborhood where the best barbecue is found, but don't dare let that stop you from giving yourself the chance to enjoy and support the work of some of the finest pitmasters in Texas.

Before my big trip, I'd occasionally had the opportunity to explore Black-owned barbecue cuisine around the state, like the famous Sam's Barbecue in Austin, but I'd always heard that the real deal could only be found in East Texas. I was excited to delve into all that Beaumont had to offer because of its reputation as the epicenter of its own style.

I also knew from the grapevine that there was a place in Beaumont called Patillo's Barbecue that I had to visit. At five generations and counting, Patillo's can lay claim to being the longest-running family barbecue spot in the state. It's a Black-owned business that began in, and then outlived, the Jim Crow era and somehow survived the race riots of 1943. For years, Jack Patillo and his wife, Roxie, had been creating unique food in their unofficial home-kitchen restaurant, along with accepting offers to cater the parties of Beaumont's wealthy, and white, elite—transcending, in some small way, the grip of segregation at the time. Soon, the Patillos had a street cart selling the beef links they became famous for (sometimes called "grease balls" in that part of the state).

In 1912, after years of growing popularity in the area, they opened their own brick-and-mortar restaurant where they've gone on to influence generations of barbecue joints that would follow their lead with the unique merging of Cajun flavors with traditional East Texas traditions that they've helped to preserve. The joining of those two flavors makes sense, but it also speaks to one of the main reasons that barbecue has endured for such a long time: its ability to so successfully and deliciously absorb so many other flavors and make something new while remaining loyal to fundamentals of the original style.

I made it to Beaumont on a Friday evening after Patillo's had closed for the day. Luckily, we were able to pull up to the outskirts of town just in time to place the last order of the day at a backroad gem by the name of Roger's

Front of Roger's BBQ Barn near Beaumont (*top*); brisket, boudin, beans, mac and cheese and cobbler from Roger's BBQ Barn near Beaumont (*bottom*).

BBQ Barn. This is a great example of one of my favorite archetypes. The type I mean is the side-of-the-road surprises that are so often found just outside a town or on a road between towns. Sometimes they stand alone, like Roger's BBQ Barn, and sometimes they'll be waiting for you in a convenience store or strip mall parking lot. They're often operated out of a prefabricated shed, which can be a cheaper alternative to the investment that a food trailer requires, and a shed with a smoker on a trailer out back can do the job just fine, assuming the owner doesn't need to be too mobile. Just like food trailers, you may find a picnic table or two out front, but just as often you'll see the locals using their tailgates or car hoods as tables. If you're in the Beaumont region and looking for a nice mix of Central Texas options like brisket along with East Texas favorites like ribs and chicken, but with a Cajun-spiced kick and the sides to match, then you'll be pleased if you stop into Rogers. If you do make it over to the Barn, make sure you try their boudin links—a tidbit of advice that really goes for any East Texas place that you see offering them on the menu. For the uninitiated, boudin is a French or, in our case, Cajun type of sausage. Traditionally, a good boudin will be stuffed with a combination of rice, seasonings and some type of meat, and in the world of Texas barbecue, the meat they choose is often brisket.

The next morning, I pulled into the parking lot of Patillo's before they flipped the sign to "Open." As the magic hour arrived, so did the first few members of a Little League team, and I followed them into the modest but cozy dining room full of checkered tables with paneled walls covered in photos, articles and memorabilia, as is common in spots like this. We placed our order, and I was chatting with Mr. Patillo as he perfected the day's batch of tea, saying, "It's got to be just right, or they'll tell me about it." That's true, you know. At each legacy barbecue spot that I've been to, a commitment to consistency and attention to those little details are some of the main ingredients in their long-lived success. Another ingredient in that success is the sense of home that you get in these places. I didn't have to ask the dad with the Little League team if he also went to Patillo's as a boy after the big game. You can pretty much bet that he did.

I'd come to Patillo's to taste the beef links, and I was hoping to also spot the historical links to the plantation barbecue roots of this region, and indeed we find them here. This is especially apparent in the meat choices, use of a thinner and an almost au jus–style barbecue sauce. The technology has changed, and the hand-dug pits are rare these days, but the connection to that history remains strong here. All the offerings, from the brisket and ribs to the sides, were delicious, but the grease bombs Patillo's is so well known

Patillo's Bar-B-Q sign, Beaumont.

for were spectacular, as expected. The pile of links was full of rich flavor, and they came out swimming in that unique house barbecue sauce. Everything on my plate was exemplative of the Cajun-fusion style that Jack and Roxie pioneered so many generations ago and that's gone on to become a staple of the area's flavor.

It was hard not to devour every morsel at Patillo's, but I was on a mission, so I had my tastes, offered my thanks, reviewed the plan for the day and headed out for the next plate. This brings up an important point that bears mentioning. If you're on a barbecue-centric adventure where you hope to make multiple stops in one day, remember that you're running a marathon, not a sprint, and that leftovers are a wonderful trophy to return home with. Take your time, just do tastings and try as many dishes as you can. One of the reasons that I like to have a friend or two with me on a barbecue adventure is that we can fill the table with more options and not miss any of the goods.

There were a couple of other barbecue spots to check out while I was in Beaumont, but one stands out above the rest, and that was Charlie's Barbecue. When I say that it stands out, I specifically mean that one of their offerings was so exceptional that I've found myself daydreaming

Drive-up service window at Charlie's Bar-B-Que & Catering, Beaumont.

about it ever since. Before I go into that dish of dreams, this brings up another important point and a great piece of advice that I've gotten again and again from barbecue experts across the state, and it's this: nothing gets on the menu by accident, and if you see a dish being offered that's out of the ordinary, you'll do well to give it a try. In the case of Charlie's BBQ, that special something is an order of oxtails.

Now, I'll be honest and admit that I've never even considered barbecuing an oxtail, but I'm grateful that others are possessed with a greater culinary imagination than I am, because I'm here to tell you, Charlie's doing something special over there in Beaumont. An order of oxtails comes piled high on a plate and, like Patillo's beef links, is swimming in sauce, but that's where the similarities end. The oxtail is sliced into medallions, each with a star-shaped bone at its center, and each nook of the star holds a delicious bite of delectable roast-like meat. Each bit is tender, savory and quite possibly addictive. I was already on my second barbecue meal of the morning, and I still broke my own rule and finished the entire plate, post haste. It didn't stand a chance of making it to the leftovers container. Everything on our table, from the exceptional links to the scrumptious sweet potato pie, was outstanding, and I can hardly wait to return.

Just to be clear, when I speak of Charlie, I'm not referring to some entity or a business name. I'm talking about the man himself. A man who puts the master in "pitmaster." After our amazing feast, I left my contact information at the register, and before we even made it to the car, Charlie had come out to catch us for a quick chat. It's hard to describe the lightning-in-a-bottle level of energy this man brings to the world. He's a passionate purveyor

Left: Charlie, owner and pitmaster of Charlie's Bar-B-Que & Catering.

Below: Oxtail, beef links, coleslaw, white bread slices and personal sweet potato pies, Charlie's Bar-B-Que & Catering.

of his craft and well respected because of it. We talked at length about the Beaumont food scene and the traditions that it held. He beamed when he heard I was from Austin, and he told us about some of his visits to the capital city—especially the time he got to take over the famed kitchen of Franklin's BBQ for a day, leading to well-deserved acclaim.

This was such a huge takeaway for me that I truly hope to impart it to you. Most barbecue restaurants exist due to the passion and cooking genius of one person or one family, and that passion brings a special level of commitment from the crew and customers. I recall Mr. Patillo joking that his coworker that day was the new girl since she'd only worked there for thirty-seven years. There are many roads that could lead a person to investing their lives into running a joint, but it's passion and love that drive them. I've seen it shining in the eyes of so many restaurant owners and pitmasters, and that goes double for Charlie. He's a true culinary artist and a restaurateur of the highest order.

Charlie's huge plates are served out of a small building with a takeout window that was likely built to be a taco shack or burger joint. Lock-down-proof takeout windows are perfect for a barbecue spot in this busy modern world, and while we were at Charlie's, the to-go line was steady. One reason for the constant business was that it was Saturday, and just like so many amazing dishes at so many must-try restaurants, Charlie only offers his oxtails one day a week—Saturday—and they always sell out early. Daniel Vaughn, the BBQ editor at *Texas Monthly Magazine*, told me that he didn't realize the Saturday rule on his first visit to Charlie's and so he made a second trip all the way to Beaumont just to try this one special dish—and was glad that he did. As if to make the point, while I was gabbing with Charlie out in the parking lot, a pickup truck rolled up, a window rolled down and a local good ol' boy leaned out to shout, "Hey, Charlie! You still got them oxtails this morning?" With a huge grin, his diamond-covered "PITMASTER" necklace twinkling in the early Beaumont sun, Charlie turned to holler back, "Yeah! We still got a few left for ya!"

Beaumont surprised me in the best ways, and I was pleased to have made it to the source of that delicious East Texas–style tradition, but this leg of my journey was just the beginning, and the region has more flavors to offer, so it was time to hit the road. While you're driving, you might get hungry for a snack, so you know what I recommend—a bite of barbecue! On many of my drives through Texas, I was pleased to find scattered along country crossroads, and especially in those spaces between regions, a wonderful archetype of barbecue restaurants that some would refer to as a "one-stop," which offers a perfect description right there in the name.

CHAPTER 2

BRYAN

As mentioned, East Texas is sparsely populated, so when there's a one-stop with nearly everything you need for daily life, folks will gladly drive for miles to get there because it's still closer than the next town. With gas, some fridges full of cold drinks, a few aisles of dry goods, a decent brisket sandwich and the possibility of running into a neighbor or two, a place like that starts to look a lot like an oasis when you live out on a homestead farm or ranch. Though we'll have others to stop in along the way, a great example of this archetype is Frank's Country Store on a back road just outside Bryan, Texas. Bryan, located in the Brazos River Valley, is a town on the cusp of Central and East Texas, but the feel of the area and the flavor of the local barbecue speaks more to the Piney Woods side, so just like South and East Dallas, we're taking the liberty of including Bryan in the eastern region on our map.

Frank's Country Store is just what its name suggests—a simple, humble and long-lived purveyor of goods and a stalwart to the community. Along the way, like so many country stores of its ilk, Frank's started up a kitchen in the back, and naturally, they began selling fresh and delicious barbecue to the locals of the area. The menu branches out to include hamburgers, sandwiches and some popular fried seafood baskets, but the three-meat plate or the chopped brisket sandwich will surely sate your hunger. If you happen to show up on an off day for the kitchen, there's no need to fret. Grab a kolache and fresh-baked cookie out of the display case by the register, grab a menu and make your plan to return for a plate every time you're near.

The dining room at Frank's Country Store & BBQ, Bryan.

While I was so near to Bryan, there was another place I had to check out. It's the place the locals take their out-of-town guests when they want to show off the flavor of home, and it's called C&J Barbeque. This is a wonderful example of an East Texas joint. The flavors and menu options in this part of East Texas find inspiration from the likes of those Beaumont treasures like Patillo's, especially with items like sauce-basted pork bellies.

Also, like most East Texas barbecue joints, they've embraced the Cajun flavors and sides of their neighbors in Louisiana, which will be abundantly clear with one bite of C&J's special chicken and sausage gumbo. Brazos Valley, the region where Bryan sits atop the Brazos River, is a border county, a cusp area between the East and Central Texas regions, so we also see a real mastery of that side of their menu as well. The brisket was right on—moist and smoky—and was that special melt-in-your-mouth kind of good you always hope for with a slice of brisket. As for the other Central Texas–inspired options, you can take their jalapeño cheese sausage as a prime example of their mastery. With a wonderful blend of flavors from spices, peppers, meat and smoke with big chunks of cheddar oozing out of each slice, C&J's would give any Hill Country competitor a run for their money.

The front entrance of C&J Barbeque, Bryan (*top*), and the dining room with the Texas flag painted on the ceiling at C&J Barbeque (*bottom*).

Brisket, ribs, jalapeño cheddar sausage, potato salad, coleslaw, pickles and onions at C&J Barbeque.

After enjoying that truly fine plate of food, I was fortunate to be able to bend the ear of Justin, the scion of C&J Barbeque. Having grown up behind the counter of one of Bryan's most beloved institutions has given Justin a unique insight into the world of Texas barbecue and what it takes to maintain a multigenerational business. What we came to in our conversation is that to be a successful spot, you need to have the foresight to evolve with the times while staying true to your roots. What's more, and I think this is crucial, a great restaurant understands that their role is to be no less than an extension of their customers' family kitchens and a second home to the generations of people who loyally pass through.

Coincidentally, though their business is centered entirely on the barbecue restaurants these days, like Frank's Country Store, C&J's began life as a gas station one-stop way back in 1982. They'd always sold brisket and beef links in the store, but in the mid-1990s, they finally took the leap and switched their focus exclusively to food and remodeled the store to accommodate their culinary pursuits.

The smoker at C&J Barbeque.

In recent years, the family added two more locations around town, but personally speaking—and perhaps this is just the history lover in me—I always like to stop by an original location whenever possible. You get the feel of what's really behind the success of a place when you visit the spot where it all began. C&J's has become a staple in Bryan for good reason. The food is delicious, the service comes with a sense of family and the ambience really fits the bill of a great Texas barbecue spot. Like a model smokehouse, the clean and well-lit dining room is lined with photos, awards and articles on every wall—all the way up to the pitched ceiling that's been painted with a giant Texas flag that covers half the room. If C&J's ain't some good ol' Texas barbecue, then nothing is.

CHAPTER 3

TYLER

I t's on the roads between Bryan in Brazos Valley and our next destination of Tyler, Texas, that we get to truly peek behind that Piney Curtain and into the forest and bayous this region is famous for. East Texas is a nature lover's dream. Whether you just take the scenic routes or go all in with camping, unbelievable diversity of flora, fauna and ecosystems awaits you in places from the Davy Crockett or Angelina National Forests to the moss-covered cypress trees of Lake Caddo or the morning fog playing peekaboo with the bass boats on Lake Palestine. But that's just to drop a few big names among the seemingly endless and often staggering displays of natural beauty that await us in East Texas. While you're working up a hunger out there, be sure to stop by places like Stringer's BBQ in Lufkin or CC's Smokehouse in Nacogdoches—both representing that mix of Cajun-inspired flavors, with traditional meats like brisket and ribs and side dishes such as boudin, gumbo and dirty rice that so clearly define the region.

Surrounded by lakes, forests and wildlife refuges, Tyler, with its nearly 106,000 residents, is the largest town in northeast Texas. While preparing for my trip, I asked a friend I knew who was originally from the area for a lead on what to try, and without hesitation, his answer was "Stanley's!" Which is to say, Stanley's Famous Pit Bar B-Q. I'm glad I took the advice because when I arrived, I found myself walking into a fine example of one of my favorite restaurant archetypes, one that we'll call a barbecue roadhouse. The big thing that distinguishes this sort of place from any other must be that they also serve their community as a bar with a music venue that hosts a calendar

The front of Stanley's Famous Pit Bar B-Q, Tyler (*top*). Brisket, ribs, turkey, coleslaw, beans and white bread slices (*bottom*).

of events. True to form, a band was setting up on stage as I delighted in my plate of food. The energy of anticipation in the room was palpable and, like smoke off the pit, rising by the moment. That's the thing with a roadhouse; it's a place where life happens. Yes, the food is outstanding at Stanley's, and their thick, fall-off-the-bone ribs alone are more than enough to win my approval, but a barbecue roadhouse holds a special place in my heart. My lifetime as a performing musician has taught me that as a tavern, roadhouses are hubs of communal connection and places to host celebrations, which practically makes them hallowed ground to a guy like me. Perhaps most importantly, places like Stanley's uniquely offer us a reason and a place to dance off that slice of pie (that we were absolutely right to order). There are plenty of these barbecue roadhouses around the state, but they're in the minority of barbecue establishments, and each one is a treasure. So don't just wait to stumble into a roadhouse; instead, seek them out and support them with your patronage as often as possible. Make sure you keep an eye on the events calendars with this type of spot so you can time your visit to really get the full experience. Enjoy that plate of barbecue, get that slice of pie and then have an after-dinner drink from the patio bar while you settle in to watch the show.

CHAPTER 4

SOUTHEAST DALLAS

A s promised in our introduction, we're including South and East Dallas in our region that covers this East Texas style, and this is because the prominent flavor of the area comes from the Black-owned barbecue joints that are more closely related to the original plantation barbecue traditions and the menus that we found in Beaumont than they are to their neighbors on the other side of the Metroplex. My choice of restaurants to share with you for this part of the trip was also one of my personal highlights—and I mean out of the whole state—and that is the one and only Smokey Joe's BBQ. This place isn't glamorous, but it's comfortable. The staff and regulars are welcoming, and the food is beyond belief. I couldn't put enough plates and sides on my table during my time there, and my only regret is that I can't visit more often.

The restaurant has been in operation since 1985, serving some of the best pork ribs, brisket, cheddar jalapeño sausages and East Texas beef links around. I honestly suggest that you splurge and try everything, but I can assure you that no matter what you pick, it's sure to knock your socks off. One of the main things that can set a barbecue menu apart from others is the sides they offer, and just like the entrées, every bite at Smokey Joe's is scrumptious. While all their sides really are stars in their own rights, there were a few that I just have to mention. For one thing, the sweet potatoes are something along the lines of a religious experience. Another side they offer that I now daydream about is the chicken tetrazzini, which is quite rare outside East Texas–style restaurants, and it puts nearly any other attempt

This page, clockwise starting from top left: 1. Smokey Joe's sign, 2. Sweet potatoes, 3. Buttermilk pie, 4. A tray with brisket, sausage, ribs, house-made pickles and onions. 5. Chicken tetrazzini.

Opposite: The smoker at Smokey Joe's, (South) Dallas.

at the dish to shame. I'm compelled to leave you with a suggestion about dessert, too. All I can say is that a single bite of the buttermilk pie from Smokey Joe's will reaffirm all the choices that brought you to that moment in your life. Gratitude is rarely more accessible than when you're enjoying a piece of their buttermilk or sweet potato pie.

Ah, East Texas, you never cease to amaze. As for you, reader, just think of all the beef links, boudin and buttermilk pies that will fill your belly in those barbecue bayous. Adventure awaits you on the far side of that Pine Curtain, but while the Big Thicket isn't going anywhere, we certainly are, because it's time we heed the advice given countless times and Go West!

WEST TEXAS STYLE REGION

HOME OF THE
TEXAS OIL FIELDS
& BOOMTOWNS

HOME TO
PALO DURO
CANYON

HOME OF
TORNADO ALLEY

INFLUENCED BY
SOUTH & CENTRAL
TEXAS REGIONAL BBQ
STYLES

REGIONAL SPECIALTY
• CHICKEN
• BEEF RIBS
• NEW MEXICO CHILIS

PART II

WEST TEXAS–STYLE REGION

West Texas. It's the home of non-ironic tumbleweeds dashing across the highways, red dirt–stained blue jeans stepping out of pickups and oil-drenched roughnecks coaxing pump jacks in dusty oil fields—though, to be fair, the area we'll consider to be representative of the West Texas style of barbecue is also home to some of our largest populations, some of the most robust financial and technology centers and some of the most thriving cultural scenes in the nation. As you may be gathering, I find West Texas to be a place of contrasts and ironies, and I'm excited to take you to some amazing barbecue stops that hold influences from all the other styles that came before.

As we discovered in the introduction, West Texas is the most recently, and still the most sparsely, populated of all the regions in the state. The region has that black gold, that Texas tea—aka oil—to thank for the few folks living out this way. That may be a minor exaggeration, but not much of one. Oil gave an incentive to settle this land that had been lacking before its discovery. It's not that it's without its splendor, perish the thought, but it's also undeniable that this can be a harsh and unforgiving land.

To illustrate this point, my mind goes to a true tale from 2012, which I remind you was the year some people believed we would all meet our demise in an apocalypse foretold by the ancient Mayans. That year, an area north of Amarillo experienced a slow-moving storm that dumped several feet of pea-size hailstones (yes, you read that correctly), along with six inches of rain. The resulting flash flood created gigantic floes of hailstones that compacted into banks of ice up to four to five feet deep on a warm summer day. A local deputy said it looked like a river of icebergs floating down the highway. That's not the only time this sort of freak hailstorm has happened out there. In 1993, Dalhart, Texas, in the upper panhandle experienced five to six feet of hailstones that, once compacted into these desert-bergs, took up to a month to melt enough to reopen some of the backroads in the affected area. That's not to mention the regular cameo appearances from tornadoes or the constant tug-of-war between frozen nights and scorching days, along with the arid nature and volatile weather inherent in this type of desert region. There's also the rattlesnakes, scorpions and centipedes, or if you prefer the larger predators, there's the ghostly wildcats or the howling, prowling packs of coyotes.

You get the gist; it can be a tough and demanding place to live, and before our modern advantages like heating and cooling technologies, well drilling and water purification technologies or regular and reliable access to long-range travel—i.e., cars and pickup trucks—it was nearly impossible to populate the area en masse. Aside from some very ingenious Indigenous tribes that cracked the code of how to thrive in the desert out west, most expansionist settlers before the 1900s endured the region only long enough to make it through to somewhere else, or at least they died trying.

In 1901, just as the Old West days of yore had come to their end, the world was turned on its ear with the discovery of an ocean of oil beneath the West Texas clay. Suddenly, there was a huge incentive to endure all the challenges offered by the region, and eventually outposts turned into boomtowns. The boomtowns that survived the twentieth century leave us the scattering of small and medium-sized towns that we see in the area today.

West Texas is an enormous part of the state by any standard, and officially, the geographical region comes in at just a hair under forty thousand square miles. Our flavor map borders draw West Texas in a totally different way than what's on a geographical map. We include parts of North Texas and all the Texas Panhandle, but we also give a large chunk of the farthest western parts of the state to our South Texas–style region. As I've said, there's a lot of interpretation going into the map of this guide, but because of these adjustments, the map reflects both the reality that you'll find on the menus and the deeper histories and connections we find around the state.

With a territory this massive, I'll focus on the highpoints of my adventure, but you'll be glad to know that there's always going to be so much more for you to discover no matter which direction you drive or how often you hit the road.

This next point wasn't on purpose, but it is notable that many of the spots that I'm sharing in this guide are found in places where the land changes from one geographical area to another or in the buffer zones that lie in the cusps of regions. In the case of this section, I find myself sharing places that we might consider gateways to the West. These are the places between places where so many people and flavors meet and where folks pause to connect. It's hard to overstate the amount of space between towns in this part of the world, and often it's the edges of West Texas that have been settled long enough to develop a few towns. I really mention all this to serve as a giant flashing neon sign of a hint, and what I'm referring to is a technique that you can use for your own personal explorations and deeper dives into this world of barbecue. Here it is in plain language: when you're trying to get off the beaten path, keep an eye out for these transition zones because if you do, you're likely to find some hidden treasures. But talk is cheap, so without further ado, let's jump right in.

CHAPTER 1

McKINNEY

Since we're dividing Dallas between East and West Texas styles, we should begin this chapter with a restaurant on the north side of the Metroplex that perfectly embodies the West Texas barbecue style. Fortunately, there's a spot in McKinney called Hutchins BBQ that fits our needs to a T. These days, both Hutchins BBQ and the town of McKinney are hot spots on the rise. McKinney was a tiny, sleepy town not so very long ago, but over the last few decades, it has experienced a healthy portion of the growth that's swept this part of the nation.

All those new residents need their barbecue, and between this location and another in the neighboring town of Frisco, Hutchins has them well taken care of. Just like Smokey Joe's, my pick for South Dallas, Hutchins also earned their spot on the *Texas Monthly Magazine*'s top 50 list in 2021, along with armloads of other honors and awards, and you can tell their success by the line of hungry diners waiting for their chance to get their own slice of heaven.

Since Hutchins offers a drive-through option, there are really two lines you can choose between: the one for cars and the one for folks like me who like to go inside and soak up the ambience. Whether dining in or taking it to go, you're going to love the smoky, juicy brisket, the thick but still tender ribs, the snap of the sausage links and the delicious sides like their brisket pinto beans, potato casserole or freshly minced broccoli salad. If you choose to dine in, you'll be rewarded at Hutchins. They offer their sit-down guests access to a free dessert bar with a banana pudding that's worthy of the finest family reunion and a peach cobbler that would make any Texan proud. Despite the

The front of Hutchins BBQ in McKinney (*top*). Stacked wood, leaned shovel and smoker at Hutchins BBQ (*bottom*).

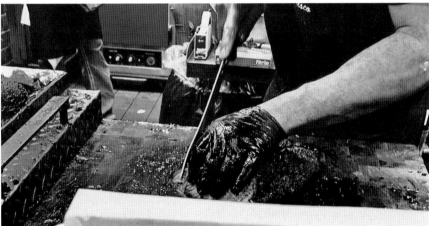

Awards line the interior entrance to Hutchins BBQ (*top*). The cutter slicing brisket at Hutchins BBQ (*bottom*).

well-deserved hustle and bustle, the staff was friendly and welcoming as they operated at full capacity during my visit, and that says a lot about a place. The influence of the Central Texas style was apparent in this "West Texas" family smokehouse. Their use of pecan and oak wood rather than mesquite is appropriate for their location on the edge of that western flavor region. Regardless of the techniques they use, the result makes their mastery of this art abundantly clear, and I'm personally excited for you to have your first taste of Hutchins BBQ. Enjoy!

CHAPTER 2

FORT WORTH

W here the West begins"—that's what they call Fort Worth when they don't call it "Cow-Town" or the "Queen City of the Prairie" or "Panther City." Regardless of the nickname, just don't call 'em late for dinner. That first description—"where the West begins"—isn't just me waxing poetic. It's a description of the area that dates to the earliest days of the city and perhaps even before. Some say it refers to a treaty-imposed border with the expanding Texas Republic that was under the leadership of a complicated Sam Houston, a man who sought a lasting peace with the Native tribes who lived in the area. One specific portion of the treaty dictated the creation of a trade house that would give the two peoples a place to establish trade, and that trading post would go on to become Fort Worth. The area west of the Trinity River was ceded to the Native tribes as hunting grounds in this treaty, and thus it was "Where the West Begins." There are other, less exciting origin stories to the motto, so I say we go with this one.

The meaning behind the nickname "Cow-Town" is fairly obvious when taken with the knowledge of the famed Chisholm Trail, which brought more than one million cows through the city from South and Central Texas. One revelation I received through my conversation with Daniel Vaughn of *Texas Monthly Magazine* was when he explained that a big reason why there ever was a cattle trade in the first place is that a person could ride down to South Texas and just gather up an ownerless herd of thin, lanky cattle that had just been living wild, and drive them north to the meat markets in places like Kansas City and, later, Fort Worth. That opportunity to build a nest egg from nothing—if you survived the trip—was a huge incentive for people in the post–Civil War South to take to the cattle trails, but we'll talk more about that later. By 1875, the West was all but won as the last of the Native American tribes of Texas had been killed or moved to Oklahoma, and by 1876, the arrival of the Pacific Railroad cemented the future of Fort Worth as a center of trade.

These days, Fort Worth puts the "FW" in "DFW," or in other words, it's half of one of the country's largest and most bustling population centers, which is referred to overall as the Metroplex. It's a testament to Fort Worth's current status as a metropolis that one of the nicknames I mentioned earlier referred to how quiet the outpost was in its early years. It's called "Panther City" because once during the days of its humble beginnings, a man of note quipped that the town was so quiet he thought he saw "a panther asleep in the street of downtown." He may have been trying to throw some shade, but what that man didn't take into account is how happy the folks around Fort Worth were to be associated with something as majestic as a panther. The people of the town leaned into the comment and turned it around to be a point of pride. I think that says a lot about Fort Worth, a community that most would consider to be the more relaxed of the sister cities. Now, I've had some amazing barbecue feasts in restaurants large and small around this area, but the one I'm taking us to now gets its name from that story, which means we're heading to Panther City BBQ.

Panther City BBQ is almost certainly going to have a line when you visit, and you should just accept that and consider it when you plan your trip. There's a good reason for the line, and it's the food, so take it as confirmation that you're in the right place and make friends with your new neighbors along the way. I assure you, standing in a barbecue queue is a great way to meet some interesting people.

I've mentioned that the defining characteristic of West Texas–style barbecue is the blending of the Central Texas style with the South Texas style, and Panther City BBQ is one of the finest examples of this fusion that I've ever had the privilege of enjoying. The spices and seasonings, entrées and sides are all perfectly reflective of the traditions and flavor of the root styles, but the result is without a doubt something different and unique. I have a feeling that played into why, out of more than 2,200 barbecue restaurants in the state, it was chosen as number 10 on that *Texas Monthly Magazine* top 50 list for 2021.

The front entrance (*top*) and the patio (*bottom*) at Panther City BBQ in Fort Worth.

I suggest you try everything on the menu at Panther City BBQ, and their incredible takes on the big three—brisket, ribs and (jalapeño cheese) sausage—can proudly stand toe to toe with any plate I've been served on my adventures around the state. I also highly recommend trying the outrageously delicious smoked mac and cheese and the borracho beans

Brisket, jalapeño cheese sausage, ribs, beans and mac and cheese, Panther City BBQ.

topped with cotija cheese, cilantro and a jalapeño slice. You'll also notice the house-made pickles and pickled onions, which, to me, usually points to a higher level of quality and attention to detail. For the record, their version of that traditional finishing touch is as delicious and worthy of praise as the rest of their menu. If you really like what they're offering, you can learn from the pros at their BBQ U—a master class for the backyard heroes—but we'll dive deeper into opportunities like those classes offered by Panther City BBQ University a bit later.

CHAPTER 3

STEPHENVILLE

outhwest of Fort Worth, where a couple of highways and a few farm-to-market roads meet, we find Stephenville, Texas. This is a unique part of the world for many reasons, but what fires my imagination is that some folks say it's here that the Spanish conquistadors, running for their lives from the revolts of the Indigenous people whom they had enslaved, abandoned vast treasures lying inside silver and gold mines. These incomprehensibly massive treasure lodes are now lost to time, but a dedicated few still search this area where the land starts to change from one form to another.

Speaking of the land change in this region, in the case of Stephenville, it's in the unique intersection where the southwestern edge of the plains and the northern borderlands of the Hill Country join up with beginnings of the vast West Texas desert that more than twenty thousand residents and Hard 8 BBQ have decided to call home. Hard 8 BBQ is a family-run, stone-pit barbecue smokehouse. Seeing those pits lined up as you walk toward the entrance tells you at just a glance that the offerings here tend to lean more toward the Central Texas influence of the West Texas style.

As with most of the spots that fall into the smokehouse side of our restaurant archetypes, we find a welcoming atmosphere with down-home vibes at any of the five Hard 8 BBQ locations that have been strategically placed in medium-sized towns surrounding the DFW Metroplex. As is my preference, I wanted to visit the Stephenville spot because it's the original, and there's just something about going to the place where it all started. Since I chose that original location, I was afforded the opportunity to speak

The wood yard and smoker pipes in front of Hard 8 BBQ in Stephenville (*top*). Smoke rolls out from the raised pits at Hard 8 BBQ (*bottom*).

Foil-wrapped briskets cooking on the raised pits at Hard 8 BBQ.

with one of the founding family members along with one of their longtime employees at length about their operation and what motivates them to make such delicious food. What it comes down to is something I've heard and felt again and again as I've crisscrossed Texas: they do it because they love it. They love being a relevant and important part of their community, and they're proud to be ambassadors of the flavors and the stories of the people who live in their region. They do it because it's important work that brings joy to the people who visit in droves every day. They do it because they're really great at making barbecue, and let's be honest—it's fun to do things you excel at.

Those busloads (sometimes literally) of people who make it to Hard 8 BBQ are rewarded with more than just friendly service and a quant dining room; they're also going to be treated to a fine Texas feast. The big standout for me as far as the food goes was the Texas-sized way everything is presented. You'll be given slabs of the perfectly marbled brisket, plump juicy sausages and thick ribs that fall off the bone. Make sure you try bacon-wrapped poppers—I suggest both the chicken and the shrimp—and don't even think about skipping the okra. I was able to make a small family reunion of my

Sausage, jalapeño poppers and an active slicing station at Hard 8 BBQ (*top*). Tray of brisket, ribs, sausage and jalapeño poppers in the serving line (*bottom*).

visit to Hard 8, and my mother still talks about their fried okra, and she's not usually a big fan of that side dish. She's right though. Their take on it is next level, so I'll throw that little tip out there to you on behalf of Mom. If you can still fit in dessert, you won't be disappointed. They have all the standards—

and I was impressed by both the berry and the peach cobbler—but they also offer their own takes on tradition, such as their whiskey buttermilk pie. I really enjoyed my time at Hard 8 BBQ. The food, the look, the tradition, the service—everything was on point while still being efficient enough to easily service the masses of happy diners that come through the door every day. If you're anywhere outside the Metroplex, be sure to stop in to one of their locations, but if you're anywhere near Stephenville, I recommend you take the time to see—and taste—the original.

As I mentioned a moment ago, being a place where roads cross, Stephenville is the sort of place you might stop on your way in or out of the town that raised me, Wichita Falls. It's known as either the home of Sheppard Air Force Base or the site of one of the largest and most destructive tornadoes to ever spin upon the plate of the world. Some know the town as the big brother of Burkburnett, Texas, the first of the oil boomtowns. But for the purpose of this guide, my suggestion is that if you're near my old stomping grounds, head to the edge of town to Iowa Park Road and check out an oasis among the mesquite trees—a barbecue roadhouse called Jordan Craft BBQ—for some fine barbecue along with a hefty serving of live music.

Another reason you might find yourself in Stephenville is on the way in or out of the Texas Panhandle, a large region all its own that also fits into this West Texas style that we're exploring. The main population centers in the panhandle are Lubbock and our northernmost city, Amarillo, both offering a touch of civilization among a vast, mostly unpopulated country that seems to stretch on forever. It may be flat as a pan in the panhandle, but that pan is atilt. Case in point: Amarillo sits at 3,605 feet of elevation. The lowest point of our hilly, centrally located city of Austin is 425 feet above sea level, while coastal Beaumont is dangling its toes only 16.5 feet above the Gulf waves.

CHAPTER 4

AMARILLO/LUBBOCK

Amarillo is another unique place where the land changes. Its flatness is deceptive, because the true character of this region lies in its depths; this is canyon country. One big attraction that might bring you to Amarillo is an adventure at Palo Duro Canyon, one of the most stunning natural wonders in the world. The canyon's depths reveal walls of endless strata that read like sheet music to a keen-eyed geologist. In some parts of the national park, each of these painted layers is a different vibrant shade of rusty red and orange, laid bare by ancient rivers that also left enormous pillars and spires that were slowly carved by its water over eons.

All that hiking through Palo Duro Canyon is sure to work up an appetite, so while you're near Amarillo, check out the barbecue scene. Whatever you choose, make sure you add Tyler's BBQ to the list, and make sure you get the ribs when you do. The owner, pitmaster and restaurant namesake, Tyler Frazer, got his chops on a pit by working for many years manning the largest transportable smoker in the world, known simply as "The Grill." It's owned by Mrs. Baird's Food and travels to all corners of the country to every expo, state fair and rodeo imaginable, and it gave Tyler all the tools he needed to make his mark on Texas barbecue. If that kind of street cred isn't enough for you, then surely the doting press, the groaning shelves full of awards or, better yet, a heaping plate of their amazing Texas barbecue will do the trick.

South of Amarillo, we find our other city of the Texas Panhandle, Lubbock. Home of 257,000 people according to the 2020 census, it's also home to Texas Tech University, which touts a student body that's more than

40,000 strong. Some might call Lubbock "Hub City" because it's the only spot for many professional services in the whole region. While you're near Lubbock, you'll likely be standing in high cotton, because this area is also the world's largest producer of that crop. Whether you're in Lubbock for some thrilling college football, the cotton bolls or just rolling through, make sure you take time to sample the local cuisine. I happen to love a good barbecue shack, so my recommendation is that you head over to a beloved local stop called The Shack. It's been feeding the folks in Lubbock since 2014, and it has earned its credentials as one of the best in the state with plate after plate of delicious food. As is more common in this region than in most areas of Texas, you'll find the fatty brisket slices and thick-cut ribs at The Shack are smoked with pecan wood as opposed to the mesquite wood of North Texas or the varieties of oak wood found in so many other parts of the state. Those little nuances, like wood choice, make all the difference and are one of the best identifiers of regional flavor profiles. Seeking out opportunities to taste the different options will lead a barbecue adventurer to some surprising treats and perhaps some new preferences. If you have your sights set on a specific spot but don't see anything about the wood they use in their smokers or pits, then just ask when you get there. Any good joint will be glad to tell you all about their process and maybe even give you a tour if they aren't too busy. If getting into the pit yard and seeing how it all works with your own eyes sounds appealing to you, then I suggest you do your best to time your visits to their slower hours—if possible. After all, some places just don't see any slow days.

CHAPTER 5

SAN ANGELO

In the Concho Valley of West Texas, an area that lies between the desert, the hills and the plains, we find San Angelo. For a town of 101,000, San Angelo is a bit of an unsung barbecue Mecca in its region, and as such, it has a surprisingly robust barbecue scene. With such stiff competition bringing out the best, you'll be hard pressed to find a bad plate of barbecue around these parts. I chose to go to one of the old-school joints in town that's been around since 1987 but has barbecue roots in the community that date back even further to around 1963. I'm referring to a humble but fantastic spot they call Smokehouse BBQ.

The Smokehouse offers a busy drive-through for takeout, or you can dine in and gab with the locals and the folks behind the counter, as I always like to do. For me, the sense of community that can be fostered in these barbecue spots is a big part of the allure. You can chat and joke and connect with the people who made your meal. If you come often enough, you'll get to know them. After some time, they'll become members of your circle, and these restaurants and smokehouses, these shacks and roadhouses, they'll become extensions of your home. Let's be honest, that's rarely, if ever going to happen at your local fast-food joint or even your swanky high-end eateries. Anywhere else, and you'll meet the hostess, the waiter, maybe the gladhanding manager, but rarely the chef, and even more rarely are all those roles filled by the same one or two people, as we often find at places like tthe Smokehouse.

The front entrance (*top*) and dining room (*bottom*) of Smokehouse BBQ in San Angelo.

Cobbler and sausage, with brisket on the cutting board (*top*). Brisket, turkey, sausage, beans, potato salad, barbecue sauce and berry cobbler at Smokehouse BBQ (*bottom*).

A custom-made outdoor smoker at Smokehouse BBQ.

Their thick, fall-off-the-bone ribs come in as the prized option here, and they tend to sell out early. You really don't want to miss out on that house specialty, so do take timing into account when you make your plans to visit, but also don't miss the turkey, which was fantastic—smoky and juicy, just like it should be. Their brisket was also deliciously flavored with the mesquite wood that is common in Concho Valley. I recommend a mix of the lean and fatty cuts, but make sure you save room for their down-home sides, because their family reunion–style green beans, potato salad and coleslaw were all on point, and their desserts, such as their peach cobbler, were terrific. The whole experience was wonderful; from the food to the down-home ambience, to the friendly family-run service, it really hit the spot. Like I said, you're not likely to have a bad plate of barbecue in San Angelo, but you're certainly going to have a great plate served along with a welcoming experience at the Smokehouse.

SOUTH TEXAS STYLE REGION

HOME TO THE
DAVIS MOUNTAINS
& BIG BEND
NATIONAL PARK

HOME TO THE RIO
GRANDE VALLEY-THE
AGRICULTURAL CENTER
OF TEXAS

ORIGINAL HOME OF THE
TEXAS CATTLE INDUSRY
& KING RANCH

HOME TO THE
MYSTERIOUS
MARFA LIGHTS &
CHUPACOBRA

HOLDS DEEP TIES TO
THE CULTURE, CUISINE,
& PEOPLE OF MEXICO

REGIONAL
SPECIALTY
• BARBACOA
• TACOS

PART III

SOUTH TEXAS–STYLE REGION

When we discuss the area of Texas that we're including as our home to the South Texas style of barbecue, we answer the age-old question: "Where's the beef?" This is because the story of these vast lands that border Mexico and stretch from our westernmost city of El Paso to our southernmost region of the Rio Grande Valley is, among other things, also the story of *vacas* (cattle), *vaqueros* (cowboys) and *ranchos* (ranches). Whereas in East Texas pork is the king of meats, it's from the Texans of the borderlands to the south that we inherit our love of beef and the rich Texan history of cattle ranching.

Before this land was known as Texas, it was called *Tejas*, a Spanish take on the Caddo word *Taysha* that translates to a variation of the English word "friend." This tidbit of etymology is why the Lone Star State is also known as the "Friendship State."

Many of the Spanish coming to the Americas as the explorers of the 1500s were on a mission to find treasure, and they pushed deep into the New World in search of legendary hordes of gold, but there were also settlers and enslaved men and women carving out cattle ranches in this new land, and they were known as the vaqueros. These vaqueros were the original horse-mounted cowboys who tended Spanish-owned cattle ranches in the Americas dating back as far as the original conquistadors' arrival in 1519. The vaqueros were made up of Moors (enslaved black Muslims from Northern Africa), Native Indigenous people, Spanish colonists and a few descendants of the boucan-barbecuing buccaneers. Their traditions thrived in Mexico, Central America and Tejas, and their influence remains foundational to the culture of the southwestern United States to this day.

It's impossible to overstate the influence of the Spanish and the vaqueros on the New World. From the horses that would help conquer the continent to the cattle of the south and the pork of the east that would feed these growing populations, all were brought and abandoned (whether on purpose or by twists of fate) by the Spanish. Each of those three animals forged unique and vital roles within these new and flourishing cultures.

As I briefly mentioned, those folks who came to Tejas, especially the vaqueros, soon mixed genetically and culturally with the Native people. It was from those unions that the Tejano people emerged. The barbacoa traditions of the buccaneers grew along with this new culture. Eventually, the word *barbacoa* came to mean a very specific type of barbecue dish—a whole cow or goat head often placed in a burlap sack and buried in coals, producing a rich, shredded beef roast. The Tejano people and their delicious traditions are still going strong in Texas, and the Tejano culture offers us a foundational ingredient in the evolution of the Texas barbecue style.

The Tejano people, still a vibrant part of Texas to this day, offer the world a connection to the buccaneers of yore and the Native tribes of the Americas like the Taino people. They are the ancestors of the Olmec, Mayan, Aztec and countless other advanced civilizations whose names have been lost to the fog of time. It was these people who created the colonies of Spain's New World empire, and for generations, this burgeoning culture lived here under Spanish colonial rule. They were building cities like San Antonio more than three hundred years ago, cultivating once-barren regions and perfecting their delectable barbacoa among a feast of other unique foods that have since swept the globe. Later, they led the revolution against Spain that spawned a free, abolitionist and democratic Mexico, and some would later choose to join their Texian neighbors as the rebels of the revolution that spawned the Republic of Texas.

In the land that the Tejano people have owned and tended for generations, the dotted lines that note national borders have ebbed and flowed like tides, and the flags above their ranches have flown, like birds, for but a season when compared to the long-held claims of these families. In many ways, this is a truly ancient land, and the Tejano people and their recipes for how to live a good life and, yes, for how to make their treasured foods are kept like sacred memories and ancient secrets.

CHAPTER 1

EL PASO

E l Paso is a fine place to delve into this rich culture and amazing style of cooking, and if you're coming into Texas from the west, it's likely to be your entrance to, and your first taste of, the Lone Star State. Among the taquerias and food trucks, your barbecue adventures will surely benefit from a long trek to this border town like no other.

The city of El Paso and its sister city of Ciudad Juarez were built on opposite banks of the Rio Grande, which is also the U.S./Mexico border. Archaeologists have found evidence suggesting thousands of years of habitation in the area, but the Spanish first set foot here in 1598, and their first settlement was built nearly one hundred years later in 1695.

El Paso lies so far away from the rest of Texas that the Republic of Texas only made its claim on this part of the map as a landgrab when it entered statehood with the United States. Most of the settlements that have grown into cities here have thrived because of the oases offered by the rivers and springs that dot the land, but these outposts are islands of humanity surrounded by vast stretches of nearly impassable desert (at least impassable without roads and cars). This physical barrier is a great way to incubate a unique flavor and style, and while you're in El Paso, I suggest you do like the locals do and try the tacos (perhaps the barbacoa) at some place like Flores Meat Market. There's also loads of great barbecue options around town, and you can't go wrong if you stop at Tony's the Pit BBQ, where they specialize in barbecue sandwiches and barbecue burritos. Their green chili salsa drives home the fact that you're not in East Texas anymore.

CHAPTER 2

MARFA/DAVIS MOUNTAINS

Another big draw to this part of the country, whether you go for the sake of your social media feed or to spot its famous and mysterious orbs of light, is making a pilgrimage to Marfa. If you head out that far into the middle of nowhere, you might want to grab a bite while you're in town and choosing Convenience West BBQ is a great call. If you've got a few friends with you, try the whole rack of ribs, and be sure to check out their green chili and cheddar beef sausages. If you're heading to the MacDonald observatory, the springs of Balmorhea or just out for some hiking in the Davis Mountains, you'll find some other fine options sprinkled around the small towns of the region, so be sure you bring an appetite along with your sense of adventure.

CHAPTER 3

SAN ANTONIO

The largest city in our South Texas–style region is San Antonio. Like so many other towns and cities in this guide, San Antonio, with more than 1.5 million residents, is a place between regions. Geographically, it sits on the southern edge of the Texas Hill Country, but we're including it as a part of South Texas–style region because, culturally speaking, the city is far more heavily influenced by its historic ties to Mexico than anything else. The history, food, architecture, culture and music all speak to those long-held connections to people of South Texas and Mexico.

Founded more than three hundred years ago, San Antonio made its mark as a world-class city in the modern age when it hosted the 1968 World's Fair, or the "HemisFair." Many of the sites that we currently enjoy in San Antonio were created in record time as part of their moment on the world stage. For example, the Hilton Palacio Del Rio is one of the world's first modular constructions, and the twenty-one-story hotel was built in around two hundred days, but the 485 modular rooms were positioned, fully furnished and ready to rent in just forty-five days. Likewise, the Tower of the Americas—the tallest observation deck in the country for thirty years after its construction—was built in just under eighteen months. San Antonio is a place of possibilities and a culture unique unto itself.

I'm frequently asked about my personal favorite barbecue picks from my trip, and I always reply that it's like choosing a favorite kid. Each place is unique and worthy of your attention, but having said that, I then usually find myself following up with a rave review and a strong encouragement to all within earshot that they visit our next stop, a place in San Antonio called 2M Smokehouse BBQ.

2M is a simple place. You're likely to find a line has formed, no matter what time you arrive, so just come prepared for that possibility. There's a reason for the line, and it passes through quickly enough. When you get to the counter, the staff make you feel like you're the first customer of the day. They were happy to take the time to answer all my questions and offered some great suggestions, too. Aside from the exceptional service (which is really saying something in the friendly world of barbecue joints), you'll also be rewarded for your short wait with an incredible meal that will leave you daydreaming about a return visit.

To describe 2M's style in brief, I'd have to say they offer craft barbecue using a South Texas flavor palate. Where in most places, even the great ones, there's usually one or two items that clearly stand out above the rest, I was honestly impressed with every single bite on my plate. I'd already heard great things about this spot before my visit, and 2M Smokehouse BBQ still exceeded my expectations. I ordered brisket with an impeccable bark; a smoky, juicy, just-right-thickness pork rib; a slice of moist, flavorful turkey; and a pork link with serrano peppers that was bursting with Oaxaca cheese.

As for sides, one thing I always look for in a truly great spot like this is if they offer their own house-made pickles. Of course, 2M makes their own pickles and go far beyond it. True to their South Texas style, their house-made onion escabeche, pico de gallo, pickled nopales (cactus), pickled spicy serranos and pickled bell peppers all left me impressed. Aside from those treats, I also had the Mexican street corn, which was perhaps the best version of the dish that I've ever eaten—creamy, cheesy and made with plump corn that left an explosion of flavor. I was all *Mmmmmmms* through the whole thing. The same goes for their chicharoni macaroni, which was a mac and cheese lover's dream and surprisingly flavorful. I recommend you let the folks behind the counter absolutely cover it in chicharróns (crumpled pork rinds) to get the full effect. It's a refreshing take on a familiar dish, and like everything on my plate, it stood out from any I've ever had.

San Antonio can be proud of the folks at 2M Smokehouse BBQ and the fine work they do as ambassadors of this world-class city, especially as masters of their craft. Judging by the sold-out sign on the barbacoa, the happy crowd in line and the impeccable plate of food that I devoured, I feel confident saying these folks seem to have struck a chord with the barbecue pilgrims of Texas, and I think you'll find it a worthy use of your barbecue adventure time, too.

The front entrance of 2M Smokehouse BBQ in San Antonio (*top*). A tray with brisket, jalapeño cheese sausage, ribs, Mexican street corn, chicharoni macaroni and house-made pickles (*bottom*).

A smokehouse with active smokers at 2M Smokehouse BBQ.

Next, we head to the southernmost tip of Texas, to the Rio Grande Valley, or as it's known around here, just "the Valley." This bilingual region has more than 1.3 million residents, and it exemplifies the unique span of border lands of our South Texas–style region that isn't exactly like the rest of America or Texas but also isn't quite Mexico either. Sitting, not accidentally, between the U.S./Mexico border and the line of highway checkpoints enforced by the U.S. Border Patrol, in many ways it's a place that's neither here nor there but somehow embodies both, and the local culture and flavors are even more complex and richer for it. The unique history of the Tejano and Hispanic people in the Valley spans nearly five hundred years, and the history of the Coahuiltecan people who came before them reaches countless generations further back into the depths of time still.

The lush farms in the Valley defy the deserts that surround them by utilizing irrigation from the Rio Grande. The long growing seasons here and the life-giving water of the river have transformed this special place into the cornucopia of Texas. The bulk of the state's fruit, vegetables and citrus are cultivated in the Valley, so we all owe a little thanks to the hard work done here to keep us fed. With a few more than 182,000 residents, Brownsville is the largest city in the Valley, and whether you're in town for a visit, stopping by on your way to Mexico or perhaps swinging through on your way to a vacation on South Padre Island for spring break or to watch a Space X launch, you'd do yourself well by taking the time to enjoy a meal at Vera's. Vera's is the one commercial restaurant in Texas that still serves the real-deal traditional barbacoa. "Real-deal," in this case, means they still use the traditional technique of burying a whole cow head in an underground pit of coals to slow roast the meat to perfection. Getting an authentic taste of this nearly lost delicacy is well worth any trouble you might go to in getting there.

CHAPTER 4

KINGSVILLE

Since our next stop is Kingsville, the support town of the gargantuan 825,000-acre (or 1,289-square-mile) King Ranch, this is a great moment to make a finer point about the connection of this area to the proliferation of cattle in Texas. To briefly recap, in the 1500s, the Spanish brought vaqueros and cattle to Texas. That was a very long time ago, and along the way, lots of fences got broken, tons of ranches were abandoned and generations of free-range, ownerless cattle lived, bred and died, all on their own without any help from humans. It turns out we may think we need beef, but cows are just fine without us. This simple point may go without saying, but it's actually a very important thing to understand on two separate levels.

First, it lets us point out that if you're a rancher, cows are a mostly hands-off stock to keep. Don't get me wrong, to keep a healthy, fat herd takes a ton of hard work, but the point remains that cows, for the most part, just want to eat. If the ranch is big enough, the cattle can just naturally roam around, grazing in a way that always keeps them fed, and that's what South Texas offers— space. The big resource here in this portion of South Texas isn't the rich fertile ground ready for farming like you find in the Valley or the plantation lands out east; instead, it's having room to roam—and graze—and lots of it.

This is a great segue into our second point, and one that my conversation with Daniel Vaughn from *Texas Monthly Magazine* helped to bring into focus. These ownerless cattle roaming South Texas didn't stay ownerless and wild for long. That means it's time to talk about those cowboys of legend from that storied time we think of as the Old West or the Wild West. This era is generally acknowledged to have been the thirty years (or so) from the end of the U.S. Civil War in 1865 to the settlement of the western territories around 1895, though there's a strong argument available to those who say it lasted quite a bit longer. During this era, the stockyards set up in conjunction with the new-fangled railroads up in Kansas City were offering good money for cattle on-the-hoof to be shipped west to feed a hungry, growing nation. Now, for those who missed out on farm life growing up, "on-the-hoof" means the animal is alive when sold to the market.

Let's put all of this into perspective. The Civil War was over, and the social contract and order of the nation had been altered in enormously impactful ways. Meanwhile, the economy of the South was in tatters. It's during these moments of upheaval and great change that we see risktakers arise and ride the waves of the turbulent social sea. In this case, it was the cowboys (and cattle queens; here's to you, Lizzie Johnson) who took the risks. In this moment, a person, regardless of the color of their skin (for the most part) and regardless of their gender (again, for the most part), could go to South Texas, wrangle up a herd of ownerless cattle that roamed free and drive that captured herd to sell in the stockyards up north.

The herds of cattle that these cowboys and cowgirls were gathering up back then weren't fat and happy like modern ranch cows. Still, skinny as these bovines might have been, they were also walking, mooing money to those folks. If a person could gather enough heads of cattle and (this part is crucial) survive the trip north to the stockyards with the cows still in tow and then repeat that feat enough times, they could potentially earn a life-changing amount of money. That was the Texas dream—that with enough luck and work, they could earn enough money to open a business, perhaps a ranch of their own. Once that person had a ranch, they might get tired of taking the risk of driving cattle or get tired of paying someone else to do it and, instead, decide to build a meat market to sell their own stock. Then maybe, just maybe, instead of letting unsold beef go to waste, that market might start smoking barbecue and selling it to the locals out of their meat market. That Texas dream has always been real and available to a lucky few, but it was perhaps never more accessible to the marginalized among us than it was in the Old West. It was a time when a whole lot of people had nothing to lose and risked it all for a better life.

To get back to the subject at hand, of all the ranches, not just in Texas but on Earth, one clearly reigns supreme, and that's the previously mentioned King Ranch, the largest of them all. Our next stop of Kingsville was founded in 1899 on land that had seen various human habitations on and off for thousands of years. The thing that happened in 1899 was that the manager of the King Ranch finally succeeded in a hard-won battle to tap into an underground lake. You see, he intended to establish a town that would be home to the ranch's business infrastructure, and tapping that aquifer meant he had the water he needed to keep that dream alive.

Today, the town of Kingsville has twenty-five thousand residents and is notably the home to a delicious barbecue spot called Bray's Smokehouse. Born of a passion for barbecue that was sparked in the firebox of their backyard smoker and now propelled by world-class barbecue skills that were honed at competitions and cookoffs, Bray's has emerged from its long genesis into a true gem of the South Texas barbecue scene. Much like 2M, this is craft barbecue at its finest, and the South Texas flavors and influence are on display and most welcome in every bite.

To get started, I recommend you at least consider going a little overboard when you order at Bray's. The menu is worth exploring, and if there are leftovers, you can just thank yourself later. This is a table service (or full-bar service) with a waitstaff type of spot instead of cafeteria style, as is often the case. Though judging solely by my visit, their takeout option is also quite popular as well.

The appetizer list should not be ignored, and it's a great way to really experience some of their more creative dishes that showcase their South Texas–style take on craft barbecue. We began with the nachos—a great choice because it was covered with in-house queso, savory brisket chili with large cubes of brisket and all the other goodness you would expect in any respectable plate of nachos and topped off with a drizzling of their avocado ranch dressing.

I also recommend their pulled pork egg rolls. Egg rolls, you say? Absolutely! Food is always evolving and fusing, as we've well established. If the world can handle kimchi tacos, then why not pulled pork egg rolls? The pulled pork, coleslaw and black bean/corn relish are stuffed into egg roll wraps and deep-fried to perfection. The flavor and texture combo are revelatory and will certainly whet your appetite for all the goodness to come.

If you're like me, the next round to come to your table will be a detour to their taco menu, because, come on, we're in South Texas here, and you've got to put some tacos on the table. Bray's offers a three-taco plate that comes with borracho beans with large chunks of sausage and a cerveza-style, all-day-appropriate, very fresh and very flavorful salsa. We got the chicken taco, the brisket taco with avocado and queso fresco and the vampire taco, which has a ton of both brisket and pulled pork, pico de gallo, jalapeños and their

Butcher's cut maps in the interior of Bray's Smokehouse (*top*) and brisket nachos and barbecue egg rolls (*bottom*).

Taco plate and beans (*top*) and chicken in the smoker (*bottom*) at Bray's Smokehouse.

delicious house-made "Vampire Sauce'" served on a "cheese crusted" flour tortilla, which is to say the cheese has been toasted onto the outside for a crispy flavor-forward experience. I certainly recommend you add that one to the list.

But wait, there's more! Don't forget we still need to get a taste of the big three, and by that, I mean their foundational brisket, ribs and sausage. From the bark of the brisket to the dense, mild sausage to the tender juiciness of their dry-rub spareribs, they've got you covered on the basics, too. We were also truly impressed with the slab of moist jalapeño cornbread that was served in lieu of the white bread you might find elsewhere in Texas. These days, many of us might associate cornbread with the Deep South, and rightfully so, but this is yet another dish given to us through our ties to those Indigenous Americans who cultivated teosinte grass into corn over countless generations. Add to that the fact that corn is one of the main crops cultivated in the region today, and it means cornbread fits in perfectly on any South Texas menu. Speaking of corn, the sweet, creamed corn was a great addition as a side. Not too soupy, Bray's allows the corn to shine through, along with some tomatoes for flavor. The coleslaw wasn't drowned in sauce either, which meant it came out to the table fresh, crisp and delicious.

I had the chance to speak with Justin Bray, one of the owners and pitmasters, to see what drives the crew at Bray's Smokehouse to deliver these high-quality plates of food and, as a result, gain the much-deserved attention of the press, the recognition of their peers and the loyalty of their growing customer base. I was pleased to see that it wasn't luck, happenstance or a glut of wealth looking for an outlet that's brought on their success. No, the thing that drives and has consistently rewarded them is passion. Passion for their craft and a passion to support their crew and their community, but also a passion to push their own boundaries in ways that make them and their menus stronger for it. I've got to say that's a list that I have a lot of respect for.

Sitting across from Justin Bray in their long-dreamt-of, thoughtfully laid out brick-and-mortar restaurant, I came to see that perhaps the thing with Bray's Smokehouse that stands out the most is that, to me, they exemplify a new path available to anyone willing to take it. This path allows a person to go from casual consumer to avid enthusiast, to backyard pitmaster, to competition chef, to food truck caterer, to brick-and-mortar start-up and perhaps hang in there long enough to one day become that decades-old legacy spot that goes on to inspire the hearts and appetites of generations of families that will come to think of this restaurant as an extension of their home. That's kind of a beautiful thought, and what could be more in line with the Texan or even the American dream than that?

CHAPTER 5

WHITSETT (CHOKE CANYON STATE PARK)

Another place between places, where the land changes and the roads cross, this time between San Antonio and Kingsville, is the area near Choke Canyon State Park and its twenty-six-thousand-acre Choke Canyon Reservoir. The Choke Canyon Reservoir is a hotspot to beat the summer heat in South Texas, and whether you need to fill up your cooler before heading to the water or just need to fill your gas tank as you pass through, you should know there's a great one-stop called Choke Canyon BBQ that has a pulled pork or chopped brisket sandwich waiting to fill your belly, too.

One-stops are a crucial part of the culture of Texas road warriors and to locals in need of an outpost of civilization alike. I've talked about this in other parts of this guide, and Choke Canyon BBQ does a great job of keeping a whole lot of Texans happy and full. The fully appointed convenience store and gas station are in a separate building from the barbecue restaurant, which I found to be a lot more appealing, while still feeling completely convenient and easy to use all the services available in the one-stop.

Speaking of easy, they serve a lot of people here, but the line moved quickly, and the food was just what we needed to keep our adventure on track. In addition to the recommended big sellers of the place, those sandwiches I mentioned earlier, we also tried out a few of the basics on the menu, and while everything like the ribs, sausage and brisket was on point, I do want to mention the notable addition of fried alligator on the menu. While not perhaps what one would expect in South Texas, I remind

The front of Choke Canyon Bar-B-Q (*top*) and a cutter selecting chicken for serving (*bottom*).

you of the earlier general rule of the weird: if there's an out-of-place item on the menu, give it a try because there's likely a good reason for it. In this case, we loved our order of fried gator, and after that first bite, the large taxidermied alligator proudly sitting on a shelf above the front door started to make a lot more sense.

CHAPTER 6

MATHIS

itting between Choke Canyon and the coastal city of Corpus Christi, we find our last stop for this South Texas portion of the guide in what, to me at least, was a surprise, under the radar, burgeoning barbecue Mecca in the small town of Mathis. I call it a burgeoning barbecue Mecca because not only is this town of fewer than five thousand people home to Butter's BBQ,—one of the 2021 top 50 spots, according to *Texas Monthly Magazine*—but it's also home to a legacy place I'd heard great things about. It's called Smolik's Smokehouse, it's been in operation since 1929 and these days they operate out of two locations. They have the newer, highway traffic–grabbing location and the original smokehouse in town that I had the absolute pleasure of stopping into. Like Butter's BBQ, Smolik's has also had its share of praise from the kingmakers at *Texas Monthly Magazine*, along with every other media outlet and right-minded diner that's crossed through its doors over the last century.

Smolik's is part traditional smokehouse (we'll dive into that in a moment), part meat market offering everything from house-made summer sausage to hand-cut steaks (which they'll happily prepare for you right then and there or wrap up to take home) and part bakery (full of all sorts of delights like kolaches, cakes, pies, cobblers, puddings, cookies, brownies and more). All those sweet treats are crafted in-house, and the cobbler à la mode that I tried was some of the best I can recall ever being served. This sentiment makes me think of the ribs Smolik's offers, so let's get to the point and talk about the smokehouse.

The front entrance of Smolik's Smokehouse in Mathis (*top*). Brisket, ribs, sausage, potato salad, beans, pickles and onions with barbecue sauce and a fresh-baked dinner roll (*bottom*).

Peach cobbler at Smolik's Smokehouse (*top*). Mike Smolik, owner and pitmaster (*bottom*).

For my plate, I had some fatty brisket, a link of juicy jalapeño cheese sausage and those ribs I just alluded to. Before we really get into this, I want to put into perspective that even though I visited Smolik's at the end of a full day of top-notch BBQ, I still couldn't resist devouring my heaping plate, which is surely a testament to their greatness. The portions are indeed generous, especially for the price point and the quality of their offerings.

Getting back to the ribs, when seeking to describe them, my mind goes straight to grandiose expressions full of superlatives, like "These ribs are what legends and happy Texans are made of!" and there's a good reason for that instinct; they were truly outstanding. I would place Smolik's Smokehouse in a class with very few peers based on their pork ribs alone. The smoke ring penetrates deep into their thick cuts, and each rich, juicy bite is better than the last, down to the creamy dab of fat that a lesser pitmaster would turn into gristle.

The jalapeño cheese sausage on offer here is another above-average offering, clearly made by folks who are masters of their craft. They use a natural sausage casing that snaps when you bite into it. For a jalapeño cheese sausage, they weren't too spicy nor too greasy, yet each bite was perfectly cheesy, spiced and smoked.

For our brisket, we asked the cutter to offer us what he thought was the best of the brisket when he asked our preference between fatty or lean cuts. He gave a bit of both, and I'm glad he did because I found the perfect bite for me included a little of both. Like the ribs, Smolik's ability to get the smoke to penetrate fully into the meat is first in class across their menu.

For our side dishes, we ordered the family reunion–style creamy mustard potato salad, along with a generous portion of fresh, delicious and not-too-soupy pinto beans. Once seated, we were also offered fresh, warm rolls with a soft and creamy house-made honey butter that melted right into the bread.

In my short time visiting Smolik's, any question about how a place could last since 1929 was answered and laid to rest. Just make and offer the world some of the best cuts of meat, some of the finest sweets and some of the best barbecue you can find in Texas, and keep doing it every day, despite the stock market crashes, wars, pandemics and rising pressures and prices from all around. Just keep that fire burning, keep those meats smoking and keep doing it the best you can. That's how you stay open for nearly one hundred years. Here's to hoping they're around for the next hundred years. I know I certainly like the idea of eating those ribs long into old age.

COASTAL TEXAS
STYLE REGION

HIGHEST REGIONAL
POPULATION &
DENSITY

HOME TO MUCH OF
AMERICA'S PUBLIC &
PRIVATE SPACE
ENDEAVORS

HOME TO MANY
HISTORIC SITES &
BATTLEGROUNDS

HOME TO ONE OF
AMERICA'S TEN
NATIONAL SEASHORES

REGIONAL
SPECIALTY

SEAFOOD

PART IV

COASTAL TEXAS–STYLE REGION

It likely goes without saying, but the Texas Gulf Coast, which is the 367 miles of real estate and public spaces along the Gulf of Mexico, is far more than just the curvy part of the distinctive shape of Texas. Home to more than seven million Texans and touting Houston (one of the largest and most diverse metro areas in the nation—but we'll get to that later) among its ranks, this is the most densely populated region in Texas.

The National Oceanic and Atmospheric Administration (NOAA) generously reports more than 3,300 miles of Gulf coastline, accounting for every nook and cranny along the way, and perhaps that count is more accurate judging by some portions of the coast where the rows of beach houses curl and stretch for miles along the sand. At the risk of oversimplifying things, it could be said that much of the coast is a series of bays and sandbar-barrier islands, and in most of these bays, you'll find towns have developed on both the coastal side and the barrier islands.

Despite so many Texans answering the siren's song of the ocean, there are still vast swaths of nearly untouched spaces that offer the safe breeding grounds needed by the Kemp's Ridley sea turtles and nearly four hundred species of birds that call the area home. A prime example is the huge chunks of North and South Padre Islands bestowed with National Shoreline status by the U.S. Parks and Wildlife Administration, the San Bernard National Wildlife Refuge or the Brazoria National Wildlife Refuge. Those spaces are all doing important work protecting the natural treasures of Texas.

The Texas coastal region has also fostered human life for thousands of years despite the regularly occurring and too often devastating hurricanes the area is infamous for producing and the local population must always stay adept at enduring. Just like any other part of Texas, the coast has its share of unique challenges posed by nature, but other than those frequent hurricanes, the long-lasting and debilitating heat and humidity, the drenching rainy seasons, the voraciously determined mosquitoes and the shark-infested waters (there are at least forty known species of sharks in the Gulf), a coastal life can be a pretty darn good way to live. One thing's for sure: in addition to the sun and surf, you can also count on finding some fine barbecue while you're going coastal.

I mentioned that the Indigenous tribes and peoples of the coast have lived in this region for eons of time, but we see the first incursions into the area by European explorers as early as 1528. That's when conquistador Álvar Núñez Cabeza de Vaca—the man who was Columbus's successor—shipwrecked near what would later become Galveston Island. Shipwrecks are a common theme along this coast, so if you're looking for some adventure, get your SCUBA gear or your metal detector and dig in!

Despite the unintended Texas Two-Step by Cabeza de Vaca, and despite the Spanish towns that would later be built, it would be the French in the 1600s who first established European-backed settlements in the coastal region, which is why the French flag is the second of the acknowledged "Six Flags over Texas."

This is admittedly a bit of a recap, but we see this French influence all over the American Gulf Coast, most notably in Louisiana but also deeply woven into the eastern and coastal regions of Texas. These days, the Francophile tendencies of America's third coast are perhaps most apparent in the food, and that, of course, includes barbecue. It's especially notable in the side dishes like gumbo, dirty rice and red beans. We first explored this French influence in our section on East Texas, and if you think back to the introduction portion of this guide, you'll recall that the coastal flavor region is a mix of the East and South Texas styles regarding traditions, seasonings and sides and touts a healthy portion of the Central Texas influence over the methods used to do the smoking.

If you're lucky (or well researched), the one thing that you might find on a coastal barbecue pit that you won't usually see elsewhere is seafood. Oh, sure you'll see some fried catfish on a menu here and there, but I'm not just talking about frying some fish out of the creek. I'm talking about barbecue-smoked seafood: snapper, seabass, tuna steaks, shrimp as big as your hand and oysters by the bucketful, just to name a bit of the bounty. I hope you're already thinking back to the Taino people and their boucans smoking seafood on green-wood racks over a pit of coals, because if you are, the idea of smoked seafood in a barbecue joint won't seem too fishy. This little quirk on the occasional coastal menu may harken back to the past, but it really speaks to the idea of barbecue as a versatile technique that is applied to whatever meat is available. The same reason why pork is prevalent in the east and beef is what's for dinner in the south and central parts of the state is why you might taste seafood on the coast—it's the meat that's available.

CHAPTER 1

SOUTH PADRE ISLAND

We just mentioned the sea turtle and avian sanctuaries and the national seashores of the Padre Islands, and since they are on the southernmost portion of the coast, let's start there. Since I have personal ties and a deep love of South Padre Island with its champion surfers, talented musicians, skilled artists and world-class sandcastle carvers, I'm honor bound to admit to my bias while still totally suggesting that if you're forced to choose between the larger North Island or the more intimate South Island, you should go south, set your clock to island time and don't look back.

As soon as you cross the Queen Isabella Memorial Bridge—the causeway that, at its height, soars seventy-eight feet over Laguna Madre—I suggest you make your way directly to Porky's Pit BBQ. Nothing is too far away on a small island, so the commute won't be a problem. When you arrive, you'll see the Coastal Texas fusion of East and South Texas influences blended into Central Texas techniques on display right there on your plate. That East Texas influence is perhaps the most apparent here with hotlinks, barbecued chicken and sides like candied yams and collard greens. Meanwhile, you can see that South Texas influence in the charro beans, and the Central Texas influence shines through in the brisket. Whatever you pick, grab enough for leftovers; that way you won't have to leave the beach for a snack later.

CHAPTER 2

CORPUS CHRISTI

The next town north up the curl from the Padre Islands is Corpus Christi, which sits where the Corpus Christi Bay meets the mouth of the 315-mile-long Nueces River. Archaeologists have unearthed evidence suggesting a long history here as a place for trade among Natives well before becoming a hot spot for smugglers running contraband into Mexico. In 1839, just three years before the Texas declaration of independence from Mexico, Colonel Henry Lawrence Kinney founded Corpus Christi or, as it was known at the time, Kinney's Trading Post. It's said that in 1840, Kinney threw the first state fair to ever be held in Texas in his new town as a way of putting it on the map.

Jumping ahead to the Civil War, from the perspective of the time, Texas was a relatively far-flung location. Because of that fact, Texas was one of the only Confederate states that, for the most part, didn't experience the flames of war in an up-close and personal sort of way, and most Texans never saw a Union soldier until it was all over. There are some major exceptions to that statement, the most obvious being the coastal port cities that truly felt the heat and the pressure of the Union embargo being enforced by the North. Due to its status as a center of trade, Corpus Christi was one of those few Texas towns that was bombarded by the Union navy—not once, but twice.

In our modern age, this port community has thrived. Today, it's home to 380,000 residents and is the eighth-largest city in the state. Feeding those folks since 1949 is a place that I highly recommend: Howard's BBQ. When you walk into this legacy restaurant, aside from the down-home vibe and the hunger-inducing aroma, the first thing you notice is their meat menu. You won't see any sides because your meal comes with complimentary access to the self-serve, all-you-can-eat, hot/cold sides and salad bar.

When you get to the meat counter, you might have a tough time deciding among the brisket, sausage, smoked turkey, smoked ham, pork ribs, beef ribs, pork loin, chopped beef, pulled pork or pulled chicken. My suggestion, of course, is that you simply try it all, but we'll also get to my personal choices in a moment.

As you greet the folks behind the counter, a crew that is likely to include the owner, you'll also likely notice the lampshades hanging over the meat are repurposed one-quart tomato ketchup cans. I couldn't resist admiring the clever decorating choice out loud, and the practiced reply came right on cue: "Thanks! We even got a free can of ketchup with each one!" That's when I knew this was my kind of place and that the man behind the counter was in fact the owner.

The restaurateur's name is Jim Matthews, not Howard. Norman Howard was the second and final Howard, by name at least, to own the place. Jim worked at Howard's for fifteen years before striking out on his own for a

The front entrance to Howard's BBQ, Corpus Christi.

Opposite, top: Brisket, ribs, potato salad, coleslaw, Spanish rice, cornbread muffin and peach cobbler.

Opposite, bottom: Turkey, sausage, green beans, ranch beans, lima beans, corn on the cob and white bread.

Above: Open hatch on the firebox at Howard's BBQ.

time. When Norman was ready to retire, he knew just who to call in to keep the business alive and man the pit into the future. Jim took up the challenge when he bought the business, and he's worked hard to not change a thing, except the occasional addition to the menu to keep up with the times. For years, he wouldn't even mention Norman's retirement, and instead, if Mr. Howard wasn't hanging around that day, he'd just tell inquisitive guests that he'd gone fishing, which was probably true.

We've brushed up against the existence of legacy places like Howard's BBQ here and there in this guide so far, but while they have many worthy peers, Howard's does a great job of naturally exemplifying that archetype of the generational family-owned and -operated joint that so defines what we've come to think of as Texas barbecue. The thing to remember here is that a business doesn't make it to the level of beloved legacy spot loyally patronized for more than seventy years without getting quite skilled at

Owner and pitmaster Jim Matthews mans the indoor smoker.

A saucy plate of barbecue with corn on the cob.

Ketchup-can lights hang over the serving line at Howard's BBQ.

making barbecue—which Howard's has done, and that's why Jim hasn't changed a thing. This is less of an "if it ain't broke, don't fix it" thing and more of an "if it's perfected, don't touch it" sort of thing.

During my visit to Howard's, the table practically groaned under the weight of the feast. There was brisket with a great smoke ring to it, served with just a touch of their rich in-house barbecue sauce. There were plump, juicy and very flavorful natural-cased sausages that rank among my personal top-ten list for sausages I had on my trek. I tried their very thick and incredibly delicious fall-off-the-bone pork ribs that would also go high on my top-ten list for best ribs. There were also a few very impressive slices of turkey in the feast that were moist, juicy and perfectly smoked, plus their fantastic pork tenderloin was another star on my plate. The smoked pork tenderloin, while not unheard of on a menu, is still a unique thing to see, and this brings us back to that pro tip about ordering the unique item on the menu because there's a reason it's there. In the case of Howard's, that's certainly true. Their tenderloin was indeed tender and smoky, juicy, and I highly recommend trying it. For a taste of the South Texas influence on coastal barbecue, you might also want to try the "Jimmy Special," which is a taco plate offering two large flour tortillas with heaping helpings of sliced brisket, sausage and chopped beef covered in barbecue sauce, and of course, it comes with access to that hot/cold sides and salad bar.

Speaking of those side dishes, they have all the bases covered at Howard's, and on the table at my visit were lima, pinto and green beans, all of which paired nicely with their spot-on Spanish rice. The boiled corn on the cob was fresh and still crisp, the cornbread muffins were ready for sopping up sauce at the end and the mustard-based family reunion–style potato salad was better than your dear old aunt makes. Their coleslaw recipe surprised me with just the right sized chunks of red delicious apples that evoked thoughts of a creamy ambrosia fruit salad, and with that small addition, a familiar staple was transformed into something delightfully new. Well, new to me, that is. It's those little touches that have kept people coming back for so long, after all.

CHAPTER 3

PORT ARANSAS

One of the best and most beloved stretches of beach on the Gulf Coast is also home to Port Aransas on Mustang Island, just off Corpus Christi Bay. In so many ways, this town is the quintessential Gulf Coast vacation spot. It is chockfull of hotels and condos, tourist shops and restaurants that bustle with the constant ebb and flow of guests between the on-season and the off-season. Whether you're there with the spring breakers seeking the party or the snowbirds escaping the cold of the great white North, you can still almost always count on finding a friendly crowd dining along with you at MacDaddy's Family Kitchen.

To be honest, I almost judged MacDaddy's by its name alone, and it wasn't the "MacDaddy" part; it was the fact that it didn't add "BBQ" in big bold letters or end with the word "Smokehouse." I'm glad I kept an open mind because what I was served on my visit was some of the finest 'que of my entire trip.

Being in the business of pleasing the tastes of wide swaths of the vacationing public, MacDaddy's wisely offers an extensive and varied menu, but even still, there's a theme at play that's in alignment with the coastal fusion of East and South Texas flavors and dishes with the Central Texas–inspired dishes and techniques. With barbecue nachos, pork chili and barbecue empanadas, the appetizer list highlights the influence of South Texas, while the basted and smoked pork spareribs, chicken leg quarters and Creole and Cajun–seasoned seafood dishes speak directly of those eastern inspirations.

Opposite, top: Palm trees tower and seagulls soar above the MacDaddy's sign in Port Aransas.

Opposite, bottom: Brisket, ribs, sausage, Brussels sprouts and jalapeño creamed corn at MacDaddy's.

Above: Fried shrimp, blackened smoked redfish, broccoli, ribs, sausage, Brussels sprouts and jalapeño creamed corn.

For my visit, I tasted smoked blackened redfish on rice with vegetables, which was nicely encrusted in seasoning, keeping it juicy and tender through the smoking process, plus the big three: their so-tender-it-falls-apart brisket with a great smoke ring and a really good bark, their delightfully smoked natural cased sausage and their pork spareribs with a sweet baste that was almost candied in the smoker. Like everything else on the table, the ribs were perfectly penetrated with smoke.

You might think, "what's the big deal with the smoke?" and all I can say is that even in a truly solid barbecue spot, I'm still sometimes left wanting a smokier flavor than I find on my plate. Smoking meat is an art and a science. The folks at MacDaddy's have perfected their craft, and it's borne out in subtle ways that leave a big impression, like imparting a consistent and deeply smoky flavor to a wide variety of meats without drying them out.

Up close and personal with a plate of barbecue, cowboy hat–clad Texan reflected in the window.

We can't go on without giving some love to the side dishes at MacDaddy's, because they really blew me away with their options. Their jalapeño creamed corn that had both jalapeño peppers and Hatch chili peppers in a creamy, practically cheesy base is at the top of my list for praise. That base sauce from the corn also happens to go great with their other sides like the rice and especially their Brussels sprouts, which were top-notch, and not just for a barbecue restaurant but compared to any kind of dining establishment. They got a good thing going in Port A, and the next time you get the chance to hit the beach, you'll know just where to go for supplies.

CHAPTER 4

ROCK PORT/MATAGORDA BAY

As we continue north up the curl from Corpus Christi and Port Aransas, we find the small, picturesque fishing community of Rock Port with just under eleven thousand residents living that sweet beach life. While I won't spend a lot of time talking about the town in this guide, you could do far worse than to spend a great deal of your time there on your next visit. I'd especially like to point to the Shack: Smokehouse and Seafood as one of those places on the coast that leans into their coastal bounty with a full barbecue menu that includes plenty of seafood options, like the seafood bomb, which is a pouch bursting with steamed fish, shrimp and vegetables, to go along with a thick slab of brisket and a pile of ribs.

One of the next bays northeast of Rock Port is Matagorda Bay, home to the town and historically significant port of Matagorda. Founded as part of Stephen F. Austin's original agreement with Mexico, it was already the third most vital port in our Gulf Coast before Texas claimed its independence from Mexico. The bay is teeming with life due to being in the nutrient-rich delta of the Lower Colorado River. At 862 miles long, the Colorado River is the longest to have both its source and its mouth in the state. It's the same river that creates the highland lakes like Lady Bird Lake in downtown Austin.

Speaking of connections between Austin and Matagorda Bay, if you go to the Bob Bullock Texas State History Museum, among the many treasures of Texas on display, you'll see a ship. Well, to be fair, you'll see the remnants of one. It's called *La Belle*, and it was shipwrecked by La Salle, the well-traveled French explorer who also explored the Great Lakes. While exploring the

Gulf of Mexico, La Salle's men ran aground in a storm. *La Belle* was lost in the bay until its discovery in 1995 by archaeologists. An enormous double steel–walled octagonal cofferdam was built to hold back the ocean surrounding the site, and an archaeological dig produced the artifacts that we see partially reassembled in Austin.

While you visit Matagorda Bay, be it for fishing, some treasure seeking or just to enjoy the beach, I suggest you take the advice I took from *Texas Monthly Magazine*, where Daniel Vaughn, in an article about his personal favorites, listed Coastal Que BBQ & More in Matagorda on a very short list of highlights from his recent trek around Texas. The temptation starts with just a cursory glance at their "Specialties," which I guess you could say is the "& More" section of their menu. That's where you'll find the options like their pork belly tacos or their Frito Gorda, which is basically their version of that old Texas favorite Frito pie, but with brisket. Another popular choice here is the chicken plates. When you come, make sure you bring some friends to share with, because you're also going to love their takes on the big three—brisket, sausage and ribs—and why choose when you can just pile it on the table and try it all? Coastal Que BBQ & More isn't necessarily a place to get your seafood fix, but if you're seeking a place to get some great Texas barbecue on the coast, look no farther.

CHAPTER 5

GALVESTON ISLAND

T hough Galveston Island was officially incorporated as a city at the beginning of the Republic of Texas in 1839, its history stretches much further back. In that history, we see the Indigenous coastal tribes that inhabited these bays for thousands of years before Cabeza De Vaca was shipwrecked here in 1528. Then we see the island being home to a settlement founded by pirate Louise-Michel Aury, who was working for the Mexican rebels fighting for independence from Spain in 1816.

In a plot twist, Aury lost control of the settlement when he returned from a raid on the Spanish to find the pirate Jean Lafitte had taken up residence there. Lafitte had just been driven from his own pirate hideout near New Orleans and found the defender-less island to be an irresistible opportunity. Lafitte would self-declare the island to be the sovereign pirate kingdom of Campeche, and of course, he also declared himself the leader of this new nation. Lafitte, our would-be pirate king, stayed on his throne until 1821. That's when he was driven out by the U.S. Navy with the ultimatum to give up the island or die defending it. Lafitte chose to live to fight another day, and he abandoned the port and torched the settlement on his way out, escaping into the night to build even more of his legend.

That port has always been a major part of the island's character and history. In the pirate years of Lafitte, human trafficking and black-market smuggling was a major business on the island, and after the island officially became part of the Republic of Texas as Galveston, the port was a major center of the cotton industry and the chattel slave trade.

That painful history of slavery here is important because it serves as the backdrop for another major historical event that happened on the island. For some context, we mentioned that most of Texas avoided major battles in the Civil War, and one result of that isolation was that word of the Emancipation Proclamation of 1863 didn't reach those held in captivity in Texas until the war was over and the Union forces sailed into Galveston Harbor. That landing was on June 18, 1865, and the next day, on June 19, U.S. Army general Gordon Granger, with his army behind him, went to various locations around the city and read the proclamation aloud, which was the first step in liberating more than 250,000 people who had been held, often for their whole lives, in captivity in Texas.

The spontaneous celebrations that erupted from those newly freed men, women and children would be the expression of joy and relief that is commemorated in the celebration of freedom known as Juneteenth. It first came to public attention as a major day of observance when Coretta Scott King chose it as the date for the Solidarity Day rally, which served as the culmination of the 1968 Poor People's March and live-in at the National Mall in Washington, D.C. In 2021, Juneteenth was lifted from a mere regional observance when it was added to the list of U.S. national holidays.

Today, Galveston Island is home to more than fifty-three thousand people, and its port is among the top fifty in the country. It's also home to a thriving tourism industry and a bountiful restaurant scene. When I asked a friend who loves to spend time on the island about their go-to spot for barbecue, there was no hesitation. It's a local's legacy spot that has been serving meals just off the beach since 1966, and it's called Queen's BBQ. It's a name that immediately invokes Galveston's original nickname from a time when its port was the busiest of them all: "Queen City of the Gulf." The locals eating at Queen's BBQ swear by stuffed baked potatoes piled high with any of their barbecue meats you'd like, but I can't help pointing out the French dip sandwich—a personal favorite dish for me, and one I can't recall seeing on any other barbecue menu. Regardless of where you wind up on the island, just be sure to enjoy all that historic Galveston has to offer—especially the 'que!

CHAPTER 6

BAYOU VISTA

There's a town on the edge of the sea that's home to little more than 1,600 people—barely more than a neighborhood really—called Bayou Vista. It's built on a series of dredged canals between the coast and Galveston Island that gives the residents of this enclave unfettered access to Galveston Bay and the Gulf. Just off the main road through town that leads to the Galveston Causeway Bridge, hidden behind a busy convenience store, is a next-level craft barbecue food truck called Smokin' Z's BBQ that put Bayou Vista on my personal barbecue map.

I really took to Smokin' Z's. Their food was creative, inventive and scrumptious. Their personal way of providing service makes you feel like an instant part of the family, and the backstory of the husband-and-wife team, Zaid and Mallory, and how they came to create one of the hottest new barbecue trucks in all of Texas is inspiring. The couple grew up just down the road in Sugarland. Mallory is a child of Canadian and American parents, and Zaid's parents came to Texas from Iraq.

It's said there's a time in every man's life when they get overly into either world war history or smoking barbecue, and even before marrying Mallory, Zaid had chosen his path and fired up the pit. He began in the backyard in his high school years after a teacher gave him a small, used smoker, and eventually he joined the competition circuit, where the couple perfected their recipes, found catering opportunities and dreamed of opening a barbecue shop. Zaid found a beat-up food truck that the couple was able to transform with some elbow grease into the welcoming little truck. After some understandable pandemic-related hiccups and delays, the truck is up and running to rave reviews, mine included.

A plate of 'que and a front-row view of Smokin' Z's BBQ in Bayou Vista.

First things first, Smokin' Z's is a small, craft 'que operation. With that in mind, if you need a large amount of food, like five pounds or more, be sure to pre-order. It's not just a great way to be courteous, but the reality is that this place will sell out of items. If you want to feed the whole crew in one stop, Z's can help you be that hero, but for the best results, you might want to plan ahead.

If you ever find yourself among the canals of Bayou Vista in the morning, I recommend you break the fast with Smokin' Z's fresh-baked brisket kolaches, and I'll add that their house-made blueberry donuts had me over the moon. As for the lunch and dinner menu, hold on to your hat, because they really deliver some impeccable dishes and sides.

With each bite, you could guess without knowing that Zain has years of experience smoking barbecue. Some of the big hits with both me and the locals are the pulled pork and the chopped brisket sandwiches served on a toasted brioche-like bun and topped with their delectable in-house pickled onions or the pulled pork tacos made with duck-fat tortillas and topped with queso fresca, cilantro, pico and tomatillo sauce. In a stroke of simple genius that had never occurred to me, they also offer brisket grilled cheese sandwiches.

"Midnight Toker," the trailer-mounted custom-made smoker at Smokin' Z's BBQ.

Smokin' Z's is in a league with very few peers. For my plate, I had a thick slab of prime-cut brisket that was moist, smoky and tender. I'd heard amazing things about the ribs, and apparently the rumors are true because they'd already sold out of them when I arrived just after 1:00 p.m. In the end, I wasn't too disappointed, because it left more room for me to enjoy one of the finest brisket boudin links I've ever been served. I love eating boudin, but if I have one complaint about the dish, it's that it can sometimes be a little too full of rice and a little too sparse with the other ingredients or spices for my personal taste, but not so with Smokin' Z's brisket boudin! Here you'll find a perfect mix of spices, vegetables and rice with huge chunks of brisket and nice smoky notes in each bite.

Of their generously portioned sides, I tasted their scrumptious jalapeño creamed corn with big, fresh kernels of sweet corn swimming in a cheesy,

Cornbread soufflé and a pulled pork sandwich at Smokin' Z's BBQ.

creamy base. I also tried their unexpected and heart-winning cornbread soufflé with a light and crispy golden-brown rise on top and whole-kernel sweet corn that I can't say enough good things about. While you're there, I'd also like to recommend you go for the loaded baked potato salad for something different.

You can see that Smokin' Z's really made a fan out of me, and I can't imagine being in the area and not stopping in. The journey Zain and Mallory have been on to get this far reminds me of when we spoke of the fellas at Bray's Smokehouse in Kingsville. I'm referring to that personal story arc that can stretch from casual diner to professional pitmaster, and it's available to those few who choose to walk that proven path from novice to competition barbecue, to catering contracts, to food trucks, to brick-and-mortar, to legacy spot. Smokin' Z's, though on its own leg of that marathon, has certainly caught its stride and even come up with some new tricks of its own. You heard it here, folks—head that way, throw a tip in the jar and grab a free beer from the cooler and dive into a picnic tableful of one of my top barbecue picks in Texas.

CHAPTER 7

HOUSTON

Houston is a tough place to write about because it defies easy definition and is always ready with an exception. We can say with confidence that it's huge. The city itself is 665 square miles and home to more than 2.3 million people, but the Greater Houston metro area is a jaw-dropping 10,062 square miles—which is an area larger than nine states—and has a combined population of over 6.6 million. To follow further down that thought, that means if Houston were its own state, it would be the thirteenth largest by population, coming in between Indiana and Missouri. If you prefer to measure by GDP, the Greater Houston area with its GDP of $512.2 billion would make it the fifteenth-largest state in the Union, coming in just below Michigan. So, yes, Houston really is quite large.

We can also say Houston is every bit as diverse as those statistics would lead you to believe. A total of 145 languages are spoken in the city, just less than New York and LA, and there are far more cultures than languages represented here. To show off all that staggering diversity, you'll find more than ten thousand restaurants representing more than seventy styles of international, as well as American, cuisine in the foodie's paradise that is Houston. It's no exaggeration to say that all manner of culinary delight awaits you around every bend.

BLOOD BROS. BBQ

The business sign on the front for brisket boudin at Blood Bros. Barbecue in Houston.

As for barbecue, you'll clearly have no trouble finding some great options, no matter what part of the city you're in. I've chosen to share a few very different stops that I made during my journey around Houston, and we'll start with one that I would easily consider among my top picks of my whole trip: Blood Bros. BBQ.

You'll see from the usually long line that word about the craft fusion barbecue wizardry that's happening at Blood Bros. has gotten out, especially since their inclusion in the *Texas Monthly Magazine* top 50 list.

The "craft" part of "craft fusion" speaks to the lengths they'll go to to achieve pecan and oak–smoked perfection with each bite and the smaller batches of meats they'll make in a day compared to some of the places that pack in the tourist buses all day. The "fusion" part refers to their combination of Caribbean, Asian and even Mediterranean flavors and dishes perfectly woven to the coastal barbecue style, which we know to be heavily influenced by the flavors and dishes of South and East Texas along with the Central Texas dishes and techniques. That's a lot of influence and inspiration, but it's a well-tuned orchestra, not a cacophony, and that speaks to the capable and creative pitmasters who mastermind it all, Quy Hoang, Jamie Valencia and Robert Wong.

In a lot of restaurants, the pitmasters and cooks might experiment with dishes and come up with a few options that are unique and delicious and keep those items on a simple menu. At Blood Bros., it's more like everything they touch is culinary gold and each dish is so unique it would be a shame not to offer it to the public. As a solution, they've curated a menu that rotates by the day, and each day is full of specialty items.

When viewed as one big picture, their vast menu spotlights a certain masterful ease with fusing wildly different cultures, styles and flavors into new yet still totally legitimate Texas barbecue dishes, and it's done with a skillfulness that lets Blood Bros. stand toe to toe with any traditional barbecue pit in the state while doing something that's all their own.

What is it that fuels their mastery in such a wide breadth of cooking styles? Aside from undeniable talent in the kitchen, it's also likely due to the three founders' early years growing up together in the culturally and

Eager diners line up for their turn at the cutting board.

Orders being filled by the expert cutters at Blood Bros. Barbecue.

A feast with heaping helpings piled high at Blood Bros. Barbecue.

socioeconomically diverse Houston working-class suburb of Alief, where they were constantly exposed to the many different cultures and delicious cuisines that Greater Houston has to offer.

Because everything on their variable menu is unique and worthy of your attention, my recommendation is that you try to get a few people together for your visit and just fill up the table with all the dishes you can; that way, you can taste as many of their offerings as possible. For my visit, I was able to take that advice, and we had a huge spread to explore. Regarding their big three, for the brisket we tried a mix of their fatty and lean cuts; both were mouthwatering, with a perfectly caramelized bark and a rich, smoky flavor. We ordered three types of their in-house sausages for the table, and all were impressive—the jalapeño cheddar sausage, a black pepper sausage and a hot link that would have been right at home coming off an East Texas pit. We also tried their thick and tender Korean-inspired sweet and savory guava-glazed pork ribs. Those core dishes were nothing less than outstanding.

We also got an order of the Thit Nuong pork belly burnt ends and a smoked char siu pork banh mi sandwich, both seamlessly drawing from a Vietnamese influence, and their Japanese-inspired togarashi split chicken.

Its crisp, spicy skin held a smoky, juicy hunk of plump meat. We also had to taste a few of their tacos. The one that stood out was the beef cheek barbacoa taco, which was tender, rich and savory.

Our crew went just as crazy ordering sides as we did with the entrées, piling the table with their delicious smoked gouda mac and cheese, their jalapeño creamed corn and their notable jalapeño coleslaw, which was crisp and creamy but with a kick. We also got their obsession-worthy Brussels sprouts, the spot-on charro beans and their fresh and juicy melon salad, and of course, we couldn't resist getting a generous portion of the aptly named ambrosia salad to round it out with something sweet, fruity and creamy.

It's hard to imagine not being impressed with the options at this restaurant, but when you get it on the table and each bite is somehow better than the last, you'll find your admiration for their skills goes to another level entirely. In a foodie's paradise like Houston, it's hard to stand out above the rest, and they've certainly figured out how to do that and more at Blood Bros. BBQ.

GOODE COMPANY BBQ

Sitting perhaps at the opposite side of the barbecue spectrum from our last stop, we find beloved Houston restaurant group Goode Company BBQ. I visited one of their newer locations that had only been around for thirty years or so, and when you enter the interior space, you'll see the decorative motif is old-timey saloon meets Texas/Old West Museum. You'll also find a wonderful example of a traditional Coastal Texas smokehouse with major

Saddles and stars line the interior entrance to Goode Company BBQ.

influences from the east and central flavor regions, and behind the counter, you'll find a friendly crew that forms a well-oiled machine, ready to serve the masses one consistently delicious meal after another.

With the brisket, smoked chicken, Czech sausage and pork ribs at Goode Company BBQ, the common standout for me was the smoky flavor of every bite, which is a gift of the mesquite wood they fire in their pits.

Top: Front view of Goode Company BBQ in Houston.

Bottom: Sausages entice those waiting in the serving line at Goode Company BBQ.

We've touched on the fact that mesquite wood tends to burn hot and fast, so it's worth mentioning that one of their slogans here is "low and slow," which isn't all that easy to do, and their ability to pull it off just goes to spotlight their many decades–long mastery of this art and science of smoking 'que.

Speaking of the entrées, to my taste, that savory brisket I mentioned was a bit reminiscent of a roast, and the ribs had a nice sweetness to their crisp

Barbecue chickens also tempt the appetite at Goode Company BBQ.

Brisket, ribs, half barbecue chicken, Spanish rice, mac and cheese, coleslaw, a slice of fresh-baked jalapeño bread, pickles, house-made barbecue sauce and an ice-cold bottle of IBC Root Beer.

bark. I'd say the smoked chicken came out on top for my plate, but I had a high regard for that smoked sausage they cook up, too.

Their traditional family reunion–style potato salad, coleslaw and mac and cheese were all solid takes on those traditional dishes, and the jambalaya rice or "Jambalaya Texana," as they call it, was the perfect nod to their East Texas influence. Goode's also lays a thick-sliced jalapeño cheddar cornbread on top of each plate that was more bread than the "cornbread" part of its name would suggest, and I thought it was a unique take on that old tradition and an unexpected treat.

We haven't spoken all that often about the barbecue sauce I enjoyed around Texas in this guide, and that's because unless it's a truly special sauce, such as what we found out in East Texas, I'd like to mostly keep our focus on the dishes. Goode & Company BBQ is one of those spots where we're going to make an exception to take a dip into their offering, because the sauce here is something else entirely and deserves some attention. It was a warm, rich, thick and creamy tomato-based sauce that if it were any different would either be some of the best tomato soup you could ever ask for or some of the best pasta sauce you could ask for, but as it stands, it is some of the best barbecue sauce you can ask for. Though it may be different from what you'll find in other haunts, it's the perfect companion to the flavors it shares a plate with.

PINKERTON'S BBQ

We find our next stop near downtown Houston, in the Heights neighborhood that sits just off that behemoth highway known as I-10, hiding behind a small sign that reads "Come and Eat It." Our destination is Pinkerton's BBQ, which also has a location in San Antonio and swings us back to that ultracraft side of the barbecue spectrum. The care they take comes across throughout their menu, including those little-thought-of items like the breakfast tacos or boudin, and does it all in a friendly, neighborhood social hub–type of environment.

From my first nibble of their extra juicy burnt ends and the peppery, fatty brisket that literally melt in your mouth, I knew we were someplace that—despite its incredibly welcoming vibe—really takes its barbecue smoking seriously. There's no way a place can produce such broad-ranging mastery like Pinkerton's delivers without that keen eye for detail and a passion for

"Come and Eat It" sign with Pinkerton's brand greets guests above the front door of Pinkerton BBQ.

A cutter in action at Pinkerton BBQ.

A well-used butcher's knife at an active cutting station.

Brisket, ribs, boudin, jalapeño rice casserole, potato salad, coleslaw and pickles.

tradition. That also came through in their fall-off-the-bone dry-rub pork ribs, which have sweet and even floral notes to them, and you can also get them mopped with their in-house glaze, which was recommended by our slicer but to my taste was unnecessary because you're already witness to a special kind of perfection with each bite of ribs as they come. I did like the glaze, though, and I'd recommend having them dress your half pulled pork and half chopped brisket sandwich with it, like so many of the regular customers do.

The side dishes maintained the bar that was set by the entrées, and on the cold side, I enjoyed their use of red cabbage in the rough-cut coleslaw with caraway seed, and I also like the hint of fruitiness that the use of apple cider vinegar brought to the recipe. I also dived right into the mustard-based caraway potato salad that delivered an unexpectedly sassy flavor and a spicy kick. On the hot side of the side dishes, I also really took to their jalapeño rice casserole, which was creamy and rich and came through with just the right level of spicy heat.

The folks at Pinkerton's are doing something special, so be sure to make a stop in and see what all the fuss is about. It doesn't take a detective to know that you'll be pleased with what you find when that plate arrives.

CENTRAL TEXAS STYLE REGION

LONGEST CONTINUAL HUMAN HABITATION IN NORTH AMERICA

KARST LIMESTONE HILLS WITH AQUIFER FED SPRINGS & RIVERS

HOME TO LEGENDARY LOST TREASURES

REGIONAL SPECIALTY
• DRY RUB BRISKET
• SAUSAGE

INFLUENCED BY GERMAN & CZECH IMMIGRANTION IN THE MID 1800'S

HOME TO THE CAPITAL OF TEXAS

PART V

CENTRAL TEXAS–STYLE REGION

We round out our trip around the Lone Star State in the epicenter of the modern Texas barbecue scene: the Central Texas flavor region. It's largely the legacy, flavors and techniques of the Hill Country that not only came to define this regional style but, in the eyes of much of the world, has come to define Texas barbecue itself.

The Texas Hill Country is a special place that I like to think of as the green jewel on the crown of Texas. It's around thirty-one thousand square miles in area, and to offer some perspective, that's just a tad larger than the Czech Republic. A big reason why it's so green here is that it's part of the Edwards Plateau, a unique eco-region that sits atop the Edwards Aquifer. That aquifer is one of the world's most productive artesian water sources. It has the task of providing hydration to more than two million Texans while also meeting the industrial and agricultural needs of the area. This is a river region with a bedrock of cave-riddled limestone sitting beneath a shallow layer of topsoil and clay. That limestone is a testament to a distant past as an ocean floor and erosion over eons. Not all the hills are from hydraulic erosion; in fact, Pilot Knob, a hill that rises above South Austin, is the remnant of a long-dormant volcano.

Central Texas and the Hill Country are home to two major metropolitan areas: the Texas capital, Austin, and the mission city of San Antonio that we've already included in our South Texas-style region. Aside from the big cities, it's also home to dozens of small towns scattered in regular frequency all over the area.

When we take a historic view and look at the legacy of barbecue in Central Texas, we find the outsized influence of a group we mentioned in our introduction: those thirty thousand or so German families who came here for a better life. Many of those folks came as part of an organized movement to create a new Germany in Texas in the 1840s and 1850s, and immigrant settlements stretched through a one-hundred-mile or so track in the hills along an old Native American path once called the Pinta Trail. Their farms, ranches and homesteads soon covered these hills, and they created the quaint towns of the region like Fredericksburg.

It's important to note that this new group of immigrants came to Texas with their own traditions of smoking meat, and they did some unique things when compared to their regional neighbors. For one, it's hard to dig a pit into rocky limestone ground, so instead, they created raised stonemason barbecue "pits" to smoke their cuts of meat. These early pits weren't constructed outside every home. They would have been built for the local meat market or on large ranches and homesteads. Very few of those stone pits still exist, as most would evolve into the large rectangular steel boxes you'll see lined up outside barbecue restaurants that opened around the region later. Another thing that was a unique contribution from this group is that they brought sausage-making equipment and techniques. Both the raised pits and the addition of sausage to the menu harken back to the Germanic roots of these immigrant families and fused perfectly with the influences and dishes they found in Texas.

As we touched on in the introduction, Central Texas–style barbecue was eventually influenced by the plantation traditions of East Texas, and after the advent of cars allowed the traversing of the nearly impassable desert, it was also influenced by the barbacoa traditions of South Texas. We also see other cross-cultural exchanges between the German settlers and the culture of South Texas/northern Mexico. I'm referring, of course, to the addition of one of Tejano music's most distinctive elements: German accordions.

These days, Central Texas is home to a dizzying amount of barbecue options, and that's just speaking of places that are specifically presenting themselves as "barbecue." You'll find ribs, brisket, smoked sausage and barbacoa on the menus of all sorts of restaurants that hold no claim to the style. These days, it seems that in Texas, barbecue in restaurants has become as pervasive as chips and salsa. There is one reason alone for this: you've got to give people what they want, and people want barbecue when they visit Central Texas. In Austin alone, there's an estimated thirty million domestic visitors (and counting) each year, and most want their taste of the barbecue scene.

There's surely a link between the somewhat recent exponential rise in the popularity of this specific regional style and the sudden rise and rapid growth of Austin as a city. There's a new and sudden visibility that Austin has on the world stage, and that attention is amplified by events like South by Southwest (SXSW) Conference and Festival that brings together hundreds of thousands of the world's leading minds—including the press corps of the world—to Austin for three weeks each spring, or the ever-popular Austin City Limits Music Festival, which also brings in hundreds of thousands of music fans each fall. That's not even mentioning the myriad other events, races and festivals—both large and small—or our musicians, tech revolutionaries, artists and political leaders who all play their parts as ambassadors for the region and the beloved barbecue ready to be enjoyed here.

Even though we'll visit quite a few places in this part of the guide, the truth is that we can do little more than scratch the surface. As a matter of necessity, there are surely even more glaring omissions in this section than in any of the others. My suggestion remains that, for the best results, you should use this guide as an inspiration and an example of how to put together your own Texas barbecue adventures. With that said, we clearly have a lot on our plate, so let's head out to the pits.

CHAPTER 1

BRENHAM/LA GRANGE

On the way out of Houston, I had hopes of checking out a highly regarded spot called LJ's BBQ in Brenham, a small town that sits about halfway between Houston and Austin, but alas, it wasn't meant to be. The all-too-familiar "sold out" sign had already been scrawled onto some butcher paper and taped onto the locked door by the time I arrived just after 1:00 p.m. It's in moments like these that it pays to have plans B and C. After all, the best way to be spontaneous is to plan ahead. With my appetite unsated, I got back in the car extra glad that I'd heard about a great little one-stop just off Highway 71 in La Grange that's called, appropriately, Texas One Stop.

Texas One Stop is a place that lives up to its name. They've got anything you might need for your car, your homestead or your appetite. There's a full general store that includes all the snacks and cold beverages you can imagine. Their house-made pickled vegetables, jellies and jams line a whole wall, and the western wear section has an impressive selection. They even have farm equipment and a few home furnishings available. All this and we're just now getting to the food counter.

I want to make this clear right up front; this isn't "gas station food" as you may have ever thought of it. This is a fantastic Czech bakery and a proper barbecue restaurant located in a place that conveniently offers other things. On my visit, I tried the sliced brisket sandwich with sauce and was impressed with the thick, tender slices and nice smoke ring. They offer a full menu, including some daily specialty items like the chicken dumplings that the locals had lined up for on the day I visited.

This page, top: A mural on the side of LJ's BBQ in Brenham.

This page, bottom: The dreaded "Sold Out" sign scrawled onto butcher paper at LJ's BBQ.

Opposite, top: The front entrance of the Texas One Stop in La Grange.

Opposite, bottom: Jars of house-made jams and preserves line a wall at the Texas One Stop.

If you can spare the time to do more than just pull off the highway, I recommend heading into town and checking out the sights. La Grange is a lovely spot that lies on a bend of the Colorado River. As with most of the state, this area has a long history with the Native Americans who lived here for countless generations, but it was established in the modern era in the 1820s. Following that, many German and Czech families made

Top: The Czech bakery is ready to sate your sweet tooth at Texas One Stop.

Bottom: You'll be able to fill all your Lone Star needs for western wear, your favorite beer or even some fine barbecue at the Texas One Stop.

their homes, bakeries and one-stops in the area in the 1840s. It offers the quintessential Texas small-town square that wraps a variety of stores around a stone courthouse sitting in the middle. It's the sort of place that rolls up the proverbial sidewalks at night, but that's not to say there's no bustle to the place. For a history lover like me, it even has a couple of small museums, such as the Texas Quilt Museum and the Texas Heroes Museum. If we're being honest though, the town is much more famous for being the home of the infamous brothel called the Chicken Ranch, which inspired the movie *The Best Little Whorehouse in Texas* and the ZZ Top song "La Grange," than it is for presenting the history of Texas quilting.

CHAPTER 2

ELGIN

The small, ten-thousand-person city of Elgin began in 1872 as a depot town named for the railroad land commissioner at the time, but folks around here think of it as the Sausage Capital of Texas. For my visit, I went to Southside Market & BBQ, which dates itself as the oldest barbecue restaurant in Texas. The business got its start all the way back in 1882, in that time before refrigeration. That's when William Moon, the company founder, was going door to door on a horse-drawn carriage with the animals he'd raised and slaughtered. If that meat didn't sell right away, there were only a couple choices about what to do with it. On the one hand, he could lose it to spoilage, or he could make sausages and barbecue it, so he got out the sausage grinder and fired up the barbecue pit. By 1886, Moon had opened his first retail meat market with smoked barbecue available in the back, and the rest is delicious history.

After all these many years, Southside Market still offers some seriously delicious barbecue with a few additions to the menu that you rarely see elsewhere. So yes, go for the thick cuts of smoky prime brisket, and obviously go all-in on their legendarily spicy original and their cheesy jalapeño cheddar sausages. Pile up your tray with plenty of their delicious family reunion–style sides and house-made desserts, but make sure you pay close attention to those special items on the menu, too. I'm referring to the sausage slammer and the lamb ribs. The sausage slammer is a big smoky, bacon-wrapped jalapeño and cheddar–stuffed sausage, which the cutter behind the counter is happy to slice into more manageable portions for your enjoyment.

The front entrance sign (*top*), ready-to-eat barbecue or meat market services available inside (*middle*) and Southside's famous sausages packaged and ready to go (*bottom*).

Lamb ribs, sliced white bread, sausage slammer, jalapeño cheese sausage, brisket, coleslaw, a pickle spear, potato salad and barbecue sauce at Southside Market.

As for the lamb ribs, I'll admit the option was new to me, and I found them to be nothing less than scrumptious. The ribs are clearly smoked low and slow. The fat of the lamb keeps the rib meat moist while the smoke and the rub work their magic. These ribs are thickly coated with spicy dry rub, and the result is a rich, tender, flavorful meat that avoids any of the negative notes that I might have once associated with lamb or mutton.

I said that lamb ribs were new to me, but they'll hardly be new to someone who grew up in the more rural parts of Central Texas, especially the Hill Country where this type of livestock is more commonly raised. Here it's more of a common tradition to smoke a lamb or a goat for spring celebrations like Easter or perhaps a pig in the fall as the families reunite to prepare for hunting season together. They'd also use parts of the pig or lamb to fatten up the lean venison into a proper juicy sausage. With that perspective in mind, it's not so surprising to see the option of lamb ribs on the menu, even if it's rare these days. Regardless, I recommend you grab an order any chance you get.

Dry-rubbed and smoked lamb ribs with pickle slices at Southside Market.

Once you've finished your meal, stroll over to the market side of the operation, where you'll find branded merch, jars of their house-made pickles, bottles of both their regular and taste bud–searing barbecue sauces and a refrigerated case of either fresh or prepackaged sausages, chickens and other cuts of meat ready to take home and throw into your backyard smoker.

CHAPTER 3

LLANO

Keeping to the theme of long-lived historical barbecue spots, next we're heading west of Austin, toward the north central portion of the Hill Country to a small town called Llano. This is the home of Cooper's Old Time Pit Bar-B-Que, which first lit their pits back in 1962. This place is famous for the "Big Chop," which is their two-inch-thick smoked pork chop that you can get served "wet," which means it's been dipped into a sort of au jus glaze.

As soon as you arrive, you'll join the friendly line that's filing toward the steel box pits sitting right outside the doors under a covered porch. Once the friendly meat cutter piles meat onto your tray, you'll head inside to the simple, memorabilia-adorned dining room that's outfitted with long rows of adjoined tables. Next, you'll add your sides, desserts and drinks and check out at the register before you find a spot among the long tables.

As for those sides, the sweet, crisp, finely chopped coleslaw and the savory green beans happily kept my attention, as did the peach cobbler at the end. The crowd around the giant barrel of their famously free pinto beans sitting next to the free loaves of bread is notable, and they lived up to the hype as some of the best in the state with their rich flavor.

The entrées were exceptional. The thick slabs of smoky brisket, juicy and peppery natural-cased sausages and tender ribs all delivered the level of quality that I've come to expect from my many visits to their downtown Austin location.

The front entrance to Cooper's Old Time Pit Bar-B-Que in Llano.

An Aggie hat and the cutting station menu in line at Cooper's Old Time Pit Bar-B-Que.

The outdoor cutting station in action at Cooper's.

Brisket, ribs, sausage, turkey, mac and cheese, coleslaw, green beans and pickles at
Cooper's.

Since I was stopping in at the original location, I wanted to try out one of their house specialties, and I was most taken with their smoked pork loin. I'm a fan of making this cut using all sorts of methods in my own kitchen, so getting a taste of how the pros smoke the dish was inspiring. My taste of this treat was tender, moist and still nicely smoked all the way through the meat. If you decide to follow my lead and get an order for yourself, then I also recommend you get yours served wet in that au jus I mentioned.

CHAPTER 4

JUNCTION

Junction, Texas, was founded in 1876 and is so named for being the point of confluence for the North and South Llano Rivers. It's also home to around 2,500 residents and Lum's BBQ. I stopped in at Lum's so I could grab some 'que to go. I was on my way to a gathering of friends and wanted to arrive a barbecue-toting hero—a pro tip, if there ever was one.

One thing that had brought me to Lum's was word of their next-level ribs, which I suppose must be true because they had already sold out of them by the time I arrived. Undaunted, I loaded up on their jalapeño cheese sausage, their so-called regular sausage and some sliced turkey that was quite moist and very smoky. Like the rest of my plate, their thick-cut brisket did not disappoint. It was a melts-in-your-mouth sort of experience, which, like the turkey and sausage, had that smoky taste permeating through each bite. When I asked the pitmaster his secret to locking in that flavor, the reason was revealed; it's that mesquite wood we've spoken of time and time again in this guide that delivers that solidly smoky flavor note.

The care taken at Lum's comes across in their house-made pickles, which were delightfully fresh and crisp. The same care could be said for their pasta salad, as well as their cool cucumber salad. I also enjoyed their creamy and crunchy coleslaw, and Lum's tangy rather than spicy barbecue sauce paired nicely with the mesquite-smoked brisket.

I also think it's worth mentioning that this is another place offering that personal favorite of mine, smoked pork loin, on their menu. You will see that option here and there, but I wouldn't exactly say it's common, so you

The front entrance to Lum's BBQ in Junction.

An homage to barbecue on the dining room fireplace mantel bookended by Longhorn and Aggie football helmets and hunting trophies, Lum's BBQ.

The smoker shack behind Lum's BBQ.

The custom smoker in the back of Lum's BBQ.

The pitmaster shows off the old raised box-pit smoker that still sees daily action at Lum's BBQ.

might want to add it to your order while you're there. Their sandwiches are also big hits, and for those you can pick one or two meat options, including their chopped brisket and pulled pork. Whether you're dining in or getting takeout, just be the one to ensure its Lum's for dinner to achieve that hero status.

CHAPTER 5

KERRVILLE

K errville lies in one of those extra special parts of the Hill Country that, according to archaeological discoveries, has sustained continuous human habitation for at least ten thousand years and likely much longer. It was named after the Texas revolutionary James Kerr, who laid out the plots in the area, but the town began as a humble shingle maker's camp before becoming a regional trade hub. These days, it's also a cultural, medical and educational center for the surrounding counties and the home to many beloved summer camps that generations of families have made part of their traditions.

This town of twenty-five thousand holds a specific and special place in my heart because it's also home to the Kerrville Folk Festival, which celebrated its fiftieth annual production in 2022. The eighteen-day, mostly volunteer-run, nonprofit, onsite camping event is the longest running of its ilk, and it's a treasure in the community of American music festivals. Many of the finest and most beloved musicians representing any number of genres have and will continue to grace its stage out on Quiet Valley Ranch, and when all those touring musicians, festival volunteers and music lovers make it out this far into the hills, you can bet they want to sample the local flavors.

That brings us directly to our next stop, Bill's BBQ. As you walk up to the cinderblock building, the first thing you'll see is the two rows of rectangular steel smokers that have been seasoning up for more than forty years—complete with stalactites of flavor hanging off the lid. Next to those,

Trucks with flags line the front of Bill's BBQ in Kerrville.

you'll see the big, relatively new tank smoker. Taken together, these wood-hungry pits have fed tens of thousands of souls, and they wear the dents and dings born from years of dutiful performance like badges of honor. Once you get a good look at the workhorses, squeeze inside to the ordering room replete with signed dollar bills stapled to the ceiling and chat with the slicers about your order. If you were a regular, they'd already know it, of course. The walls throughout Bill's are covered in unframed photos of friends, family and the once famous who have come to visit over the years. There are also plenty of newspaper clippings about the restaurant and the region and any number of wonderfully weird and kitschy items. This being hunting country, you'll also be greeted by all manner of taxidermized hunting trophies hanging on the walls, including two literally unbelievable specimens, namely a chupacabra and a jackalope.

Ambiance aside, the real action is on the plates or in the party-sized orders that you might want to pick up to feed a whole crew. If feeding a group is on the agenda, they've got you covered at Bill's. On my visit, I was able to get a peek of a whole, split pig that was fresh off the pit. It was a special commission that had been smoked to order for a loyal customer. Everyone working at Bill's BBQ prides themselves on that sort of personal connection with the regulars and locals and in carrying on the traditional methods that have earned them more of the loyal following they've enjoyed for more than forty years.

This spot was built in the 1960s as a location for Cooper's (that beloved barbecue joint that we visited back in Llano), and that's when the big

An "open" sign greets you in the smoke shack entrance at Bill's BBQ.

Inscribed dollar bills are stapled to the ceiling, while memorabilia and hunting trophies (including some of a cryptozoological nature) line the walls at Bill's BBQ.

Owner and pitmaster Joe Marino Jr. seen through the smoker at Bill's BBQ.

boxy smokers out front first came into use, but the family that has been operating Bill's BBQ got the place in 1982. That was Joe and Dee Marino, and their son Joe Jr. runs the pit and owns the business these days. He came back to the family business after a stint as a graphic designer in the glory days era of Austin and has been making barbecue magic out in the Hill Country ever since.

The plates at Bill's BBQ are best described as solid, traditional, Central Texas–style 'que with picture perfect family reunion–style sides and amazing homemade pies that change with the seasons. If the buttermilk pie is available, I highly recommend it. The brisket comes with a good, flavorful bark and a deep smoke ring, and the sausage is juicy and smoky and made with natural casing. The barbecue chicken was a huge highlight for me, and I know it to be a real favorite among the regulars. Those family reunion–style sides I mentioned—including their creamy coleslaw and mustard-based potato salad among the cold sides or their pinto beans representing the warm sides—were all delightfully above average in every way.

Bill's also offers, somewhat uniquely these days, cabrito, which is their slow smoked take on the roasted goat recipe from traditional Mexican cuisine. Cabrito can be too fatty if it's prepared wrong, but the methods employed at Bill's result in a mild, smoky and relatively lean version that avoids being too greasy. This is a great dish to sample if you want to leave the normal menu and explore the edges of traditional Hill Country and Central Texas–style barbecue at its best, and Bill's BBQ is just the place to do it.

CHAPTER 6

BOERNE

A mid the waves of organized German immigrants coming to Texas in the 1840s and 1850s, there were also smaller subsets of organized settlement such as the agnostic (or atheistic), staunchly antislavery, progressively (and passionately) intellectual German Freethinkers (or *Freidenker* in the mother tongue). They created the towns around Kendall County such as Boerne, Comfort and Sisterdale. These days, Kendall County is considered by *Progressive Farmer* magazine to be one of the top five "Best Places to Live in America," and if you ask the Texas State Historical Association, they'll tell you it's also "the only rural stronghold of agnosticism in the state of Texas."

The seat of this unique county in the hills is Boerne, which was founded by the Freethinkers in 1852 but by the time of this writing has grown to nearly twenty-two thousand residents, which is more than double the number of folks living here a decade ago. Despite all the growth, there's still a deep connection to the long-running businesses that have supported the town for so many generations, such as our next stop, Klein Smokehaus.

The Smokehaus has changed names over the years, but the families behind the business have been cutting meat in the butcher shop at this location since the 1950s. In 2021, the torch was passed to yet another generation looking to keep the operation open and growing for the next seventy years. They're well positioned to pull it off, too. Klein's does a brisk business in wholesale meat processing, local deer and small game processing, as well as a thriving public-facing meat market/butcher shop with an impressive

The front entrance and side mural of Klein Smokehaus in Boerne.

For years, you could always take your bag of barbecue to enjoy at home, on your truck's tailgate or on your car's hood, but a dining area is coming soon to Klein Smokehaus.

barbecue operation attached. The barbecue has been takeout-only forever, but the new operators are opening a dining room option—a good sign of the growth of both the town and the business. But let's talk about why so many folks are stopping in.

First, and perhaps foremost, the flavor of the green oak smoke used at Klein's deliciously permeates their barbecue menu. Their brisket—by which I'm referring to their thick slabs of smoky, tender beef—was all the better for it, as was their nearly two-inch-thick, pepper-barked, pork chop–like spareribs, and the same goes for their house-made, natural cased sausages. The unique, smoky notes they pull off here really set it all off in the best way. They start a big fire on Monday and use those same coals throughout their various processes all week. This gives a level of continuity of flavor to every bite, no matter the type of meat, a feat that can be tough to accomplish otherwise.

The side options are also special at Klein's. The cold broccoli salad includes thin slices of carrots, cranberries and sunflower seeds in a semi-sweet sauce. It was also nice to have the chance to try a chunky, red-skinned, mayonnaise-based potato salad for a change. If you're loyal to the traditional mustard-based potato salad, you needn't worry; they offer both, along with some serious dessert options. Of those various seasonal pies and cobblers, I highly recommend you get a taste of the buttermilk pie. It's truly exceptional, and I want another slice every time I think about it.

CHAPTER 7

DRIFTWOOD

Driftwood is a funny place. There's not really a town to this town, yet the area that has "Driftwood" in its postal address has become a real hot spot as the closest place for the people of Austin to access the famed wineries and event spaces and the barbecue of the Hill Country. If you're not from Texas, parts of that last sentence might have given you pause, because there's every chance you don't know about the Texas wine scene, since export out of the state is complicated at best.

Wine production in Texas dates all the way back to the work of Spanish missionaries near El Paso in the 1650s. The wine crops that came in the centuries that followed were decimated during American Prohibition, and the industry didn't even begin making a comeback until the late 1970s. Today, there's more than 4,500 square acres dedicated to wine production in Texas, the fourth-largest wine scene in the country, producing around two million gallons (or ten million bottles) of wine annually. More than any other region in the state, the wineries of the Hill Country have skillfully crafted their picturesque wine production spaces in ways that also allow them to serve as beloved wedding and event spaces. In the process, they've created an alternative income source for these family operations and a whole new type of cottage industry for the region.

Long before the wineries and the subdevelopments popped up all over this area, there was a popular barbecue spot called Salt Lick BBQ that has reigned supreme around these parts for generations. They say they can and do serve more than two thousand people a day. As a tour guide in Austin,

I have personally taken untold thousands of people to Salt Lick over the years, and I can't recall anything other than glowing reviews from each guest. The rave reviews aren't just from the casual diners, either. In fact, Salt Lick has won nearly every award and honor and topped every list compiled to recognize excellence in barbecue.

The big hits here are the tender brisket, with a well-defined smoke ring and a peppery bark, and their fall-off-the-bone tender pork ribs with a sweet, sticky bark. If you have a few people with you, I recommend the family-style option which is all-you-can-eat brisket, ribs and delicious, peppery sausage. That will also come with endless vinegar-based chunky potato salad, rich beans and thick-cut vinegar-based coleslaw. I also recommend that you try out the juicy and tender smoked turkey at Salt Lick or go all in with their turkey sandwich. While you're there, make sure that you tap into your sweet tooth and try their house-made chocolate pecan pies and their cobblers; both the peach and berry varieties are out of this world.

The family-owned operation has grown organically over the decades since firing up their first circular brick pit in 1962. Today, the Driftwood location has twin buildings with matching pits and expansive dining rooms in each.

This indoor circular pit with hood found at Salt Lick BBQ in Driftwood is nothing less than hallowed ground for a Texas barbecue adventurer.

You'll also find copious amounts of outdoor seating options; a "kids' ranch" outdoor play area; a butterfly garden with a fountain; a bocce ball court; an outdoor pizza oven; a blue, selfie-ready, Tardis-style "Dr. Who" call box; and a separate wine tasting room with full bar—a helpful option. But here's another pro tip: the restaurant is officially BYOB, and you're welcome to tote in your cooler. If you do check out the bar, you might notice Salt Lick Red and Salt Lick White wines are available by the glass or the bottle. It's their own collaborative label made in conjunction with other local wineries. It's no surprise they got into the wine game; after all, the property also includes a vineyard. It's out by the helicopter landing pad.

These days, Salt Lick has expanded with a second location that's brilliantly located in the parking lot of the popular Round Rock Express AAA Baseball Stadium, as well as a third location in the Austin Bergstrom International Airport, showing their status as an iconic Austin-area business and a leading ambassador for the region.

CHAPTER 8

SAN MARCOS/NEW BRAUNFELS

The area shared by San Marcos and its next-door neighbor, New Braunfels, is a very special region. Today, San Marcos is the home to some sixty-eight thousand residents (and growing), and New Braunfels is slightly larger with nearly eighty thousand residents. The main similarity between the two towns can best be described with two words: springs and rivers.

Just like in Kerrville, archaeologists believe that this place accounts for some of the longest-running human habitation in North America. The reason for the deep history here lies with natural springs pouring millions of gallons of crystal-clear water from Edwards Aquifer into the formation of the stunningly beautiful rivers. In San Marcos, it's Aquarena Springs creating the San Marcos River, which is such an important feature to the people of this area. They've chosen the mermaid as one of their mascots and have ten lovely mermaid statues of various designs strategically located around the city to greet the thousands of college students attending Texas State University.

In the case of New Braunfels, it's the Comal Springs that give rise to one of the shortest rivers in the world, the Comal River, which runs for just three miles before lending its waters to the Guadalupe River. This river means so much to the locals that Schlitterbahn, one of the world's most unique water parks, created on the Comal River, has become the city's number-two employer.

I mentioned the San Marcos River, the Comal River and even the Guadalupe River all winding through this area, but there's another "river" of sorts that runs through these towns. I'm referring, of course, to that constant stream of traffic known as Interstate Highway 35 (aka I-35), which stretches nearly all the way from Canada to Mexico and almost fully bisects Texas. Hundreds of thousands of motorists use the highway in this part of Texas every day, and with that many people coming through, there's no better place to create one of the largest convenience stores in the world. It sits just between a couple of the largest outlet malls on the planet, the Tanger and San Marcos Premium Outlet Malls, and that popular water park we just mentioned, Schlitterbahn. The place I'm referring to, and our next stop, is that beaver mascot–touting oasis on the highway, none other than Buc-ee's, the Texas-sized 66,335-square-foot behemoth one-stop.

In recent years, Buc-ee's has opened even larger operations than this one around the country, but for a long time, this waystation on the northern edge of New Braunfels was the undisputed end-all-be-all of one-stops. It's also notable that this is not a truck stop. Oh, it's a gas station. With 120 fueling stations, you can be sure of that, but the big rigs aren't allowed at Buc-ee's unless they're dropping off the seemingly infinite merchandise on sale inside and out.

Buc-ee's is absurdly big on every level, and this location takes up an eighteen-acre footprint with one thousand parking spots. Its famously clean, award-winning bathrooms include eighty-three stalls. There's every Texas-themed (or Buc-ee's-themed) souvenir you could ever imagine, along with everyday goods of all sorts, from fresh foods to some impressive grills and smokers lined up for sale around the outside of the building.

Chief among that fresh food selection is some impressive barbecue being served to hungry travelers every day. This being a travel stop, the big sellers are the chopped or sliced brisket sandwiches or the smoked sausages that are served either on a stick or as a wrap in a tortilla, all of which I've personally enjoyed many times. You'll be forgiven if you're surprised to hear that the barbecue at Buc-ee's is actually pretty good, especially when we put into context the sheer volume produced in their pits every day. It's one thing to offer the world a spectacle to behold, and Buc-ee's has unquestionably done that. But it's another thing to consistently back up the schtick with quality offerings, yet Buc-ee's pulls it off, day after day—a testament to their dedicated team. It's an impressive thing to see such a well-oiled machine operating seamlessly through the throngs of people coming to get a glimpse, and taste, of the biggest one-stop in Texas—and a selfie with a beaver statue, of course. It's certainly worth heeding their many, many billboards and stopping in to give it a try.

CHAPTER 9

LOCKHART

S outh of Austin and east of I-35, the small town of Lockhart is the "BBQ Capital of Texas," and that's not just local bluster. It was officially pronounced as such in a resolution passed by the Texas House of Representatives in 1999 and then by the Texas State Senate in 2003. That's due in no small part to the fact that despite the small size of the town, you'll find six of the most highly regarded, award-winning barbecue haunts in this one barbecue Mecca.

BLACK'S BARBECUE

The tourists all know about Black's, which has been working hard "8 days a week" since 1932 and has spawned several beloved family-related offshoot restaurants in the region, and it's a great spot with a lot of well-earned clout, connections and history. The thick, juicy ribs, peppery sausage with a great snap and perfectly smoked brisket show their role as a top-tier legacy barbecue spot, and you'll be glad you stopped in for a visit.

"Open 8 Days a Week," seen on the front entrance of Black's Barbecue in Lockhart.

A platter of brisket, ribs and sausage, with green beans, Spanish rice and sweet potatoes at Black's Barbecue.

Kreuz Market

The tourist buses also know Kreuz Market, which offers a near religious experience as you enter past the coin-operated claw machines, standing in line in a covered but not air-conditioned portion of the building with big windows letting you look inside at the people already enjoying their meals in the brightly lit, climate-controlled dining room. The temperature rises with each step closer to the pit room, especially if you visit in summer.

When it's your turn to enter the meat room, you find a hazy sanctuary where the light is muted with the yellow smoke that's escaped from the rows upon rows of rectangular brick and steel pits. Take it all in and step toward the counter that sits like a semicircular altar in the middle of the room. There, the pitmasters guide you through your order with the efficient assurance that only comes with years of practice, not unlike a priest teaching a familiar prayer.

Laden with a pile of barbecue tucked into butcher paper origami, you head into the bright light and cool air of the dining room. There, you pick up your sides and find a table to dive into your feast. Head swimming from the cool air and access to oxygen, you'll take your seat and look out to the line of initiates waiting for their turn before the high priests (or are they the shamans?) of barbecue. Perhaps I exaggerate the experience, but if I do, it's not by much.

Opposite: The woodyard with a water tower and agricultural infrastructure in the background at Kreuz Market.

Above: The front entrance (*top*) and the cathedral-like smoker room with pitmasters, slicers and customers (*bottom*) at Kreuz Market in Lockhart.

A cutter fills an order at Kreuz Market (*top*). Brisket, ribs, sausage, creamed corn, mac and cheese, white bread slices, beans and potato salad, with a sleeve of crackers and a fountain drink in a souvenir cup (*bottom*).

SMITTY'S MARKET

In 1948, a longtime friend and employee of the Kreuz family, Edgar "Smitty" Schmid, bought the original Kreuz Market town square location to start his own meat market and restaurant. It may be smaller than Kreuz Market, but it was all Smitty needed to blaze his own trail and open one of the finest barbecue spots in the state, Smitty's Market.

Fortunately for us, Smitty's hasn't changed much at all since he first opened. There's still a meat market counter in operation, but these days, the barbecue is in higher demand than ever. It's a place so good they barely have a sign out front. Even without hanging much of a shingle, the aroma of smoked meats and the well-earned reputation for excellent barbecue will likely be more than enough to lure you in.

Be aware of one important thing before you arrive at Smitty's Market, and this is something that isn't all that uncommon in the world of Texas barbecue: this place is cash only. Not to worry; there's an ATM on the way inside. Just make sure you withdraw plenty on the way in so you don't lose your place in line when you see the wares and want a taste of everything.

Brisket, ribs, sausages, barbecue sauce, green beans, coleslaw, potato salad and white bread slices at Smitty's Market.

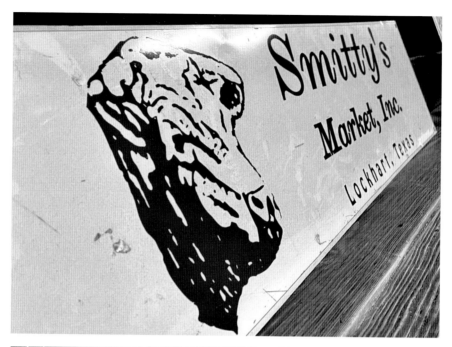

A metal sign (*top*) and a view into the pit room being manned (*bottom*) at Smitty's Market in Lockhart.

Being a smaller operation means more attention can be lavished on every ounce of meat that passes through their pit, and the result is truly spectacular. The brisket is moist and tender, with a great smoke ring, and the sausage is plump, juicy, smoky, peppery and some of the best I have been served anywhere in the state.

The same goes for their outstanding pork ribs, which, even though they were nearly two inches thick, still fall off the bone with a tenderness and sweet smokiness that won't let you put one down even for a moment. These are exceptional specimens of what pork ribs could and should be. The smoke ring and coloring of their ribs is nothing less than a work of art, and the sweet bark is in perfect harmony with the juicy, savory meat.

The sides lived up to the same high standards as the entrées, such as their green beans, which were the broad and flat variety, and rich with loads of butter. The coleslaw was crisp and creamy and better than you might even have hoped for, and let us never omit their potato salad, which had something akin to the flavor found in a French onion dip. Smitty's Market is certainly doing its part to carry the weight of the barbecue crown of Texas.

CHAPTER 10

AUSTIN

Austin is another tough place to define, but for its own unique reasons. In the case of Austin, the challenge is that it's experiencing such a mind-boggling pace of growth and it's all happened in such a short amount of time that it's hard to say what, exactly, Austin is today or what it's becoming. As is always the case, it's much easier to say what it's been: a haven for artists and the counterculture of the South, the home of the hippies who kept the summer of love alive, a hidden cultural enclave at the foot of the hills, a technological hub, an educational center. All of the things that Austin has been hiding are becoming clear to the world, even as some parts of that magic mix, like the anonymous, small-town life that was once offered here, disappear. Austin is in flux, a work in progress—a place with a rich past that is very much still becoming whatever it will be.

Don't get the wrong idea; it's still all the things it once was: musical hot spot, shining cultural beacon, bastion of liberalism smack in the middle of a conservative Texas, foodie oasis that's full of natural treasures and home to a welcoming, creative community. But it's also becoming much more as it grows into its new life as a metropolis with a present population that tops one million residents in the city and well over two million residents in the Greater Austin area.

Since Austin is growing like a weed, it's good that we have such a robust food scene to feed us through it all, from humble old neighborhood food trucks on the southside like Tres Marias to Uchi, the famed Michelin-starred brainchild of Tyson Cole, the chef who was awarded the James Beard

A Lone Star–adorned capitol perimeter fence in foreground and Texas State Capitol dome in the background, located in downtown Austin.

Foundation's title of "Best Chef in the Southwest" in 2011. More than food trucks and more than fancy sushi restaurants, Austin is known for its many topnotch barbecue spots. No matter what side of town you happen to find yourself when hunger strikes, even in the airport (I'm looking at you, Salt Lick BBQ), you needn't go far to tame your appetite with some of the best barbecue around.

Austin offers nearly every archetype of barbecue restaurant that we've talked about so far in this guide, and maybe even a couple more. We have the roadhouses that offer live music, such as Green Mesquite near Barton Springs, or even famed Stubbs BBQ holding court in the downtown Red River Cultural District. Stubbs is best known across the country for its widely distributed barbecue sauce, but it's favored locally for hosting amazing performances by prominent local and touring musical artists in its backyard outdoor amphitheater and for its beloved Sunday gospel brunch. That's when they host bluesy, soulful gospel music, performed on their indoor stage during a delicious and heaping barbecue-centric brunch that's set up in a buffet style. By the way, securing reservations ahead of time for this very popular weekly event is highly recommended.

We have the craft barbecue food trucks—and lots of them—top of that field being LeRoy & Lewis, which sits behind the hip and fantastic Cosmic

Coffee + Beer Garden. I've been a fan of this little craft fusion barbecue truck-that-could since they first opened their service window in 2017, and I was glad to see their inclusion in the top 10 of top 50 barbecue spots chosen by *Texas Monthly Magazine* in 2021. It's a well-deserved honor given to a friendly and very creative crew that is doing whole new takes on very familiar things, such as their beet-based barbecue sauce and their mustard barbecue sauce or their vegan (yes, vegan) cauliflower burnt ends or their— get this—cheddar cheesecake with Ritz crust, apple butter and cheddar crisps. Amazing! I mentioned some of their more unique items just then, but all the favorites—like Akaushi brisket, Citra hop pork sausage, beef cheeks and barbacoa—are there, just as you'd expect, and every item is incredibly well made at that.

Austin also has a few historic barbecue shacks around, like Sam's BBQ, known for its tagline "You don't need no teeth to eat my meat" and for serving thick, juicy ribs, plump, smoky sausages and piles of tender brisket, along with the rare inclusion of mutton on the menu.

We have one-stops like Rudy's, which not only offers gas and the usual convenience store fare but is also a beloved barbecue restaurant with a loyal following. If you're ever near a Rudy's BBQ location in the morning, make sure you swing through to pick up a few of their hearty barbecue breakfast tacos.

It should come as no surprise that Austin hosts many traditional barbecue smokehouses, such as the long-open Iron Works BBQ near the Austin Convention Center or the very popular Terry Black's BBQ, located on Barton Springs Road. In case you're connecting the dots to our visit to Lockhart, yes, this is one of the restaurants opened by the extended Black family. When you make it to Terry Black's BBQ, be sure to ask for a tour of the pit house out in the parking lot, and if you don't miss out on the pork ribs while you're eating there, you won't leave disappointed. Items can sell out fast here, so make sure to come as early as you can fit into your schedule.

Austin is also home to some great craft barbecue, such as Stiles Switch, which has quickly become a darling of the Austin barbecue scene. You'd do well to pick this spot to try a beef rib, which, to me at least, is reminiscent of that portion of the *Flintstones* opening scene when the plate of dino ribs tips over Fred's car. The point is that beef ribs really are quite large, and they can be tough and chewy if not prepared properly, but they've mastered the art and offer a terrific take on the beef rib at Stiles Switch BBQ.

The capital city of Texas is also home to one of the most famous barbecue restaurants in the world, and that would be none other than

Live oak trees line the front and side patios (*top*) and the wall menu behind the bar (*bottom*) at Loro Asian Smokehouse & Bar.

Aaron and Stacy Franklin's sensation, Franklin's BBQ. This now-vaunted restaurant hails from humble beginnings as a simple food truck. It rose to worldwide fame in the July 2011 issue of *Bon Appetit* magazine when the editor of the magazine called it "the best barbecue in the country." Soon, the rich and famous followed suit with a spotlight on Anthony Bourdain's *No Reservations*, followed by attention from every other food and travel show

Fried wonton chips served with Thai green salsa and peanut sambal (*top*) and oak-grilled snap peas (*bottom*) from Loro Asian Smokehouse & Bar.

Chicken karaage with chili aioli (*top*) and oak-smoked salmon with cucumber-yuzu broth (*bottom*) from Loro Asian Smokehouse & Bar.

and magazine. There was a prominent cameo in the major motion picture *Chef*, and it was even honored with a presidential visit by Barack Obama while he was in office.

Like Tyson Cole, that chef from the sushi phenom called Uchi, in 2015 Aaron Franklin was also honored by the James Beard Foundation as the "Best Chef in the Southwest." I've circled back to Tyson Cole for good reason, and it's because he and Aaron Franklin decided to put their heads and their menus together to create our last spot to visit on our trip around Texas. It's a place that might well be showing us one possible future of barbecue in Texas, and that's the craft fusion masterpiece called Loro Asian Smokehouse & Bar. Loro is a sensory experience like no other set inside an elegantly designed and tastefully decorated location that was purpose built for the endeavor on bustling South Lamar Boulevard, just south of Lady Bird Lake and Zilker Park and not far from Tyson Cole's sushi hotspot, Uchi.

Loro is truly something else and always offers a hopping social hub even beyond their wildly popular and surprisingly generous happy hour. The service is top tier, with a knowledgeable staff that is truly happy to educate a curious guest with not just an explanation but even a sample of a dish that's caught their eye.

Every trip to Loro must begin with their take on chips and salsa, which is their practically addictive fried wonton chips with Thai green salsa and peanut sambal for dipping. And don't miss adding an order of candied kettle corn with the Japanese togarashi pepper, sea salt and brisket burnt ends. Both are surprisingly munchable, even if you've had them before.

The crunchy sweet corn fritters, topped with cilantro and served with a zippy sriracha aioli, are crisp yet creamy with big kernels of corn and come to the table piping hot. The Texas sweet corn is another must-try dish that is as visually beautiful as it is delicious. The dish is made with yuzu kosho (Japanese citrus and chili paste) aioli, Sriracha powder, sunburst tomato and cotija cheese and is topped off with a crucial squirt of lime wedge just before being devoured. The colors, aromas and tastes of the sweet, creamy, citrusy and spicy flavors of this dish all combine into a truly next-level culinary experience.

While we're off and exploring the less-barbecue side of the menu, be sure you try the chicken karaage, which comes out in big, plump nuggets of chicken covered in Thai herbs, Szechuan salt and a spicy chili aioli for dipping and goes quite nicely with the coconut-scented rice with hints of lemongrass and is served with lime leaves.

Smoked beef brisket (*top*) and smoked babyback duroc pork ribs (*bottom*) at Loro Asian Smokehouse & Bar.

Getting to the meat menu, we see some more familiar sights, though they come with what by now should be some expected twists. We'll start with their smoked beef brisket, which they prepare with a chili gastrique (a type of sweet and sour sauce) and Thai herbs. It's not only presented like a piece of art, but each bite of the juicy, smoky and entirely unique brisket is *Mmmmmm…* inducing.

Next, I'd like to put your attention onto their exceptional smoked babyback duroc pork ribs. Duroc is an older—and these days lesser-known—breed of pig. These ribs are served with some gorgeous and delicious pickled cauliflowers and green onions. The bark is sweet and crisp. The smoke perfectly complements the sweet and spicy flavors while deeply penetrating the meat, and every bite was a tender, juicy and impeccably prepared treat.

The smoked prime bavette, which *Texas Monthly Magazine* will tell you is a "fancy flap steak" (and Aaron Franklin's favorite cut of beef), is a true masterpiece. This dish is nothing less than extraordinary, and it's prepared with great care. First, the bavette is salted and cold smoked. Then, excess brisket fat is cubed and put in a pan that is placed beneath the brisket that is roasting in the rotisserie so the chef can catch the drippings. Once collected, bavette is submerged in that mix of prime brisket fat and drippings in a ninety-minute sous vide bath before being grilled in post oak coals and sliced into thin ribbons for plating with Shishito pepper, salsa verde, cilantro and house-made pickles. The result is a notable and special dish that is worthy of fawning over.

I also want to take a moment to recommend the char siew pork belly with its sweet, spicy and sticky hoisin sauce. This dish is tender, juicy and savory beyond words, and the flavor combinations will transport you directly to your happy place.

No, Loro Asian Smokehouse & Bar is not your traditional Texas barbecue spot, and that's the point of my spotlighting it. As we've laid out in this guide time and again, barbecue is a living cuisine, and while its well-defined traditions provide it with a firm foundation on which to build, it's in the ability of barbecue not just to absorb other styles but to celebrate the fusion of far-flung and wildly different cuisines that gives barbecue its way of staying relevant to so many different groups of people hailing from so many parts of the world.

I said in the beginning of this guide that the history of barbecue isn't a story of unification, but after driving so many miles, eating so many plates of food and meeting so many (and such different) people, it pleases me to say that perhaps a story of unification could be in the future of this cuisine.

Peach-yuzu cobbler with five-spice whipped mascarpone at Loro Asian Smokehouse & Bar.

That's why I wanted to wrap up here, in a place where two of the best chefs in the world have taken two of the most popular cooking styles in the world (Asian cuisine and Texas barbecue), and together they've come up with something different, fresh and that is their own unique culinary expression undeniably built on those foundations we've spent so much time exploring in this guide.

Just like Austin, Loro offers unexpected twists on the old familiar themes of Texas. When you plan your trips around the state, just make sure you try the new and the non-traditional as well as the tried and true, and be sure to set aside plenty of time for an in-depth exploration of this Austin food scene. If you do, I can assure you that your Texas barbecue adventure will be all the better for the time spent. Quite simply, it wouldn't be complete without it.

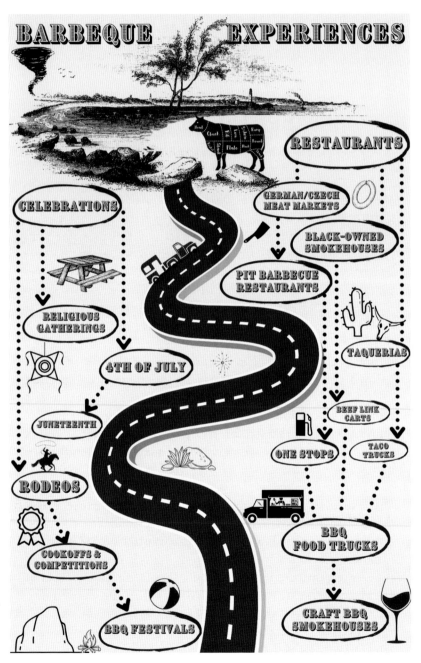

Broad view of the barbecue world, with examples of celebratory barbecue events on the left side and connections between restaurant archetypes laid out on the right.

PART VI

CELEBRATION, BACKYARD AND COMPETITION BARBECUE

We've spent most of our time in this guide discussing and exploring restaurant barbecue, but if you think back to our introduction, you'll recall that I described this as a tree with two main branches. Restaurants obviously make up one very important limb, but the other equally relevant and even older part of this tree is celebration barbecue.

When I refer to that term "celebration barbecue," I hope it evokes not just thoughts of the big parties of life but also of those intimate backyard affairs, because we really are speaking of any non-professional barbecue endeavor (I think it would be unfair to use the word "amateur" here) when we speak of celebration barbecue. As we'll discuss, this could include any number of occasions, from holidays or reunions to birthdays, quinceañeras or bat mitzvahs. It could be a rodeo, a festival or a barbecue competition. There's really no bad reason to throw a barbecue. It can even help put the "fun" back into "funeral"! (I beg your pardon, reader; I was simply dying to make that joke.)

We've mentioned that the development of barbecue was a response to need. It evolved from those shallow-trenched boucans smoking fish over coals into a way to feed a large group of people, and clearly celebratory feasting is one of the main times when that need for barbecue arises. With that in mind, it makes perfect sense that we see barbecue intricately woven into holiday traditions such as Easter, Labor Day and Memorial Day, and of course, barbecue is central to Juneteenth emancipation celebrations, as well as any self-respecting Independence Day party. It's the perfect food for so many occasions that if we all decided to recognize a brand-new holiday tomorrow, you can bet we'd fire up the smokers and serve barbecue for that new observance, too.

On a smaller scale, barbecue also serves as the perfect way to observe those smaller and more intimate moments such as a birthday, wedding or family reunion. That versatility and adaptability is what makes this method of food preservation so popular among so many different groups of people, and it's a big part of what allowed barbecue to endure. Think for a moment of all the talented chefs and pitmasters who have influenced barbecue and think of all the cultural influences that have been fused together to create a plate of Texas-style barbecue. Yet, despite centuries of evolution, the basic heart of the process has mostly remained the same. That's a testament to both the genius and the simplicity of the method. It is a medium for culinary artists, a canvas on which any number of masterpieces can be painted.

Another reason that barbecue has endured as a cuisine is its accessibility. You can get real fancy with barbecue, and if you want to start buying the latest and greatest gear, tech and new-fangled smokers, I've got good news for you—they'll let you spend as much as you want out there. But remember that this is a cuisine that can be accessed with little more than a shovel to dig a pit, a stack of stones or some sheets of scrap metal. I've seen someone convert a broken-down washing machine into a smoker. The point is that with a little imagination and a can-do attitude, a pit or a smoker can easily be bought, built, dug or slapped together by nearly anyone, no matter the budget. I would add, just so that it's been said, that if you do take to building your own setup, you should always remember to place safety first and take every precaution to avoid property damage or personal injury. You're playing with fire here, after all, so take care. There are endless resources available that teach about how to build these pits and smokers properly, and they can be found online or at your local library and bookstore.

There will always be a few challenges for the budding backyard pitmaster, but many rewards await those who take the journey. Luckily, there are some folks who are there to help, like the "BBQU" offered by the folks at Panther City BBQ in Fort Worth. Any good barbecue class will cover all the basics, including how to choose and maintain a smoker, wood and meat selection, trimming and seasoning methods, pro tips and tricks and, of course, cooking and slicing methods. These comprehensive intensives can set a beginner on the path to becoming a future pitmaster. With a little knowledge and a lot of practice, becoming a backyard barbecue hero is in reach for nearly anyone.

Once a person feels like they've mastered their own takes on the barbecue basics, they might want to share that hard-earned skill with the world. Maybe they'll take over the pit for that big family reunion or pull off some magic for that church fundraiser. If the food is well received, and if they're endowed with that drive to prove they're the best, a person might decide to throw their brisket into the ring or get a group of friends together as a team to join the world of barbecue competitions.

In Texas, there are two main competitive barbecue organizations: the International Barbeque Cookers Association (IBCA) and Champions Barbecue Alliance (CBA). Both are committed to promoting Texas barbecue chefs and barbecue culture through friendly and fair competitions that are hosted in communities, large and small, in every corner of the state. No matter where you are in Texas or what time of year it is, there's likely a competition and a related festival coming soon to a field, parking lot or 4H barn near you. They're often part of an annual county fair, rodeo or larger barbecue festival.

A great way to get involved with barbecue competitions is to start by attending. If you like the energy of the events and want to go further, then take the next step by becoming a judge. For a small fee, you'll take a short class that teaches you the rules and methodology of barbecue judging before setting you loose to help pick a winner. There's no better way to see what you like and don't like and to learn what wins competitions than to be the one tasting it all. After honing your palate as a judge and trying out your own recipes and techniques at home, you can sign up for your first competition already knowing how to win.

Whether or not you go into competitive cooking, if you decide to get into the barbecue lifestyle on any level, you'll need to set up your cooking station. This can seem overwhelming, because in today's market, there are countless options. Even though you'll need to educate yourself on the ins and outs of whatever specific models you're choosing between, I can at least help you clear up some of the clutter involved in the decision.

To narrow things down, let's start with the basics. Decide whether you prefer a stationary, built-in smoker or if you think you'd prefer a portable model. For example, if you rent a house with a small yard, you may not want to dig a giant barbecue pit—at least not without permission from the landlord. In a case like that, perhaps something a bit more portable would be appropriate. If a permanent, built-in structure would be the perfect complement to the patio of your dreams, then the right pit for you may not be sitting in the lineup outside Buc-ee's.

Now that you've figured that out for yourself, hold onto your pick while we talk about the other major difference between smoker types, which is all about the heat. Namely, whether to opt for a vertical or an offset smoker (or some modern combination of both). Both have their pros and cons, but the difference is simple, even if the shapes and sizes vary.

An offset smoker has a heat source—usually a fire box—positioned next to, but not inside, the cooking chamber. In this type of oven, the food is slow roasted through the hot or cold smoke (depending on your preference) that is channeled from the fire box into the cooking chamber, and that allows more time for the smoke to penetrate the meat. These can come in all manner of shapes and sizes, but of the portable variety, a common type looks like a barrel laid on its side with a hinged lid cut into it and a small fire box attached to the end of the barrel.

A vertical smoker is also true to its name. In this setup, the heat source—be it wood coals, charcoal, gas or electric—is positioned in the bottom of the cooking chamber, and green wood, pellets or some smoke-producing material is placed above the heat source. Above that, you may add an optional cooking stone and/or a tray of water at the bottom of the chamber that is used to regulate and even out the temperature in the cooking chamber. Above that, you find the grates for holding meat, or a rotisserie spit, positioned for cooking. In a vertical smoker, the cooking is done by the heat source on the bottom, and smoke can be added or not as desired for flavoring.

That's really all there is to it. For the most part, it all comes down to countless variations on those two themes—vertical or offset heat and whether the contraption can be moved or not. Now you'll be able to see past all the gadgets and gizmos and choose an option that fits your lifestyle and makes the kind of barbecue that you prefer.

Celebration barbecue, be it for a party, a competition or the backyard, is some of the purest and most traditional ways to enjoy this cuisine. It allows us to peer back through the smoke of history and be in touch with the countless generations of unnamed chefs, cooks and pitmasters who have contributed to this cuisine. All of it is connected in one way or another, and all of it is available for you to explore on your own terms.

Engaging barbecue in these celebratory ways will connect you more deeply to your restaurant-centric adventures around the state as well. Bear in mind that almost every single one of those professional pits was first lit off the spark of a personal passion for barbecue. That spark was nursed into the flame in the celebrations and the backyards of their lives, until one day they finally decided, for whatever reason, to bring that passion to the public with their own food truck or restaurant. The more you eat and cook barbecue, the more you'll see the connections between the dishes you're served wherever you go.

These days, Texas-style barbecue has left the state lines. The more you look, the more you'll find that touting the barbecue flavors of the Lone Star State has become big business all over the country and the world. After all the miles I've traveled, all the plates of barbecue I've devoured and all the friends I've made along the way of writing this guide, it's easy for me to see what all the fuss is about. If you want to find out for yourself, you should now have nearly everything you need to know to get out there and start ordering like a pro or even smoking your own barbecue like a pro, along with a few good suggestions of where and just how to get started.

ABOUT THE AUTHOR

Jason Weems, author of *A History Lover's Guide to Austin*, is the "Face of Austin," according to the local visitor and convention bureau. Longtime Texan, passionate tour guide and lover of barbecue, to his thousands of tour guests, Jason is renowned for breathing life, levity and accessibility into the stories of Texas. An award-winning singer-songwriter, voice actor, podcaster and event/festival producer, Weems has honed his skills as a weaver of tales and spinner of yarns over a lifetime of live performances and through years of providing immersive guided tours, in person and online. For more information about the author, please visit www.jasonweems.com.

Visit us at
www.historypress.com